Economics of Petroleum, Principles

Economics of Petroleum

Principles

By

Roshdy Ebrahim, Ph.D

Copyright © 2018 Roshdy Ebrahim

All right reserved

ISBN: 9781980391074

Preface

As the power source of social developments, energy is of decisive importance to a country's economic performance, competition ability and overall national strength. Among all kinds of energy, petroleum and natural gas, functioning as the key resources, high-quality chemical raw materials and indispensable war materials, are capturing more and more attention nowadays by counties all around the world, that is why they are also called the black gold.

Only when human societies started to utilize the fossil fuels, with their high levels of energy density, was the limit upon their size and complexity removed. The Renaissance and the resulting scientific revolution may have stretched that limit, but without the utilization of fossil fuels they could not have broken free. With fossil fuels, the change in the energy available was revolutionary, driving the rapid changes to human civilization over the past two centuries. The ratio of energy gained to energy spent for the fossil fuels was at least 80:1 for coal, 100:1 for oil, and 18:1 for natural gas. Also, the sheer volume of the energy that could be utilized dwarfed that which was previously available. Prior to this, the rate of energy use was limited by the depth and fertility of the soil, together with the vagaries of the weather. Now humanity had access to many millennia worth of photosynthesis which had been transformed into energy-dense substances and stored away under the ground. The only limitation was how quickly these new energy sources could be extracted. Naturally, the easiest ones went first. This huge increase in available energy has been the basis of modern industrial societies, which in turn have become addicted to this seemingly endless supply of cheap energy.

Fossil fuels (coal, oil and natural gas) provide about 87 % of the energy utilized by humanity, and modern societies are completely dependent upon this massive amount of energy to maintain and grow their size and complexity. Among the fossil fuels, oil takes a special place, not only providing about 33 % of global energy, but also being the predominant transport fuel given its energy density and liquid form at room temperature. Since the exploration, extraction, and transportation of the other fossil fuels are themselves heavily dependent upon the availability of oil, a shortage of oil could easily lead to constraints on the supply of all the other fossil fuels. Coal, gas, and even plants (such as corn and sugarcane) can be used to produce something like oil but much of the energy is used up in the conversion process. In the foreseeable future, these processes will not be able to significantly offset declines in oil production as there are severe limitations on the rate at which the required facilities could be put in place and the scale of production that they could support. Some transport sectors could be converted to use electricity, but the huge infrastructure and vehicle changes needed would require significant amounts of the declining net energy supplies available. History demonstrates that large scale energy use transformations have taken many decades to complete. Thus, if global oil production falters, or even falls, within the next decade, economic growth will almost certainly grind to a halt.

Natural gas is currently the number three fossil fuel in terms of share of the global primary energy mix and for years the world has debated the potential for natural gas to play a critical part in building a more resilient and sustainable energy future. While the demand outlook is currently uncertain, advances in supply side technologies for unconventional resource development, led by advances in US shale gas operations, have changed the supply landscape and created new prospects for affordable and secure supplies of natural gas.

contents

contents 6

Introduction 8

1. What Is Energy? 13
   - Main Sources of Energy on Earth 22
2. What is hydrocarbons 31
   - 2.1. Sources of Hydrocarbons 31
   - 2.2. The Formation of Fossil Fuels 35
   - 2.3. Earth's Carbon Inventory: Its Origin and Abundance 43
     - 2.3.1. Earth's Major Carbon Reservoirs 43
     - 2.3.2. Origin of Carbon Fuels: Biotic vs. Abiotic   46
   - 2.4. Hydrocarbon Systems (Saudi Arabia as an example) 49
3. What Is Petroleum? 61
   - 3.1. source and reservoir rocks 70
   - 3.2. Over thrust belts 73
   - 3.3. Petroleum Fractions 78
   - 3.4. Well Type 85
4. Concept of Crude oil 87
   - Classification of Crude Oil at the Surface 105
5. Concept of Natural Gas 111

- Classifications for Natural Gas 125
6. Conventional and Unconventional Resources..127
    6.1. Tar Sands or Extra Heavy Oils 150
    6.2. Non-Conventional Oil and Gas......155
    6.3. Properties of Unconventional Crude Oils   162
    6.4. Difficulties Associated with the Use of Unconventional Oils...............................166
    6.5. Oil Shale 168
        6.5.1. Oil Shale Classification...........173
        6.5.2. Availability of light tight (shale) oil   179
    6.6. Tight Gas (or Shale Gas) 180
    6.7. Energy return on energy invested.202
7. Peak of the Global Production of 'All-Oil', and 'All-Liquids' 210
    7.1. Global Estimates............................212
    7.2. Oil Forecasts Prior to 1956 212
    7.3. The Second Half of the Oil Age......214
    7.4. Hubbert's Peak 216
    7.5. Peak Oil and Related Issues 228
References 241
Biography of the author.................................245

Introduction

Crude oil and natural gas (mostly methane but including some longer-chain hydrocarbons) have been used by humans for thousands of years for a variety of purposes including lighting, heating, and medicinal uses. However, use was limited by access to natural seeps of oil and gas and the available technologies to extract and store the products. The earliest known oil wells were drilled in China in the fourth century using bamboo. It was not, however, until the mid-nineteenth century that large-scale production began, when metal piping allowed deeper drilling into hard rock. Early commercial production began in Poland and Romania and this was followed rapidly by drilling successes in the Russian Empire, in what is now Azerbaijan, and in the United States. Development of the process of fractional distillation at this time fueled the demand for crude oil, which could now be economically refined into kerosene for use in oil lamps. The development of the internal combustion engine also created a demand for oil and this greatly expanded with Karl Benz's invention of the gasoline powered automobile, patented in 1886. The transport sector became the dominant user of oil and currently accounts for 61.4% of oil consumption. Other major uses include lubrication, chemical feedstock, and domestic heating. Production has risen dramatically over the last century and production of crude oil today is approximately 73 million barrels per day (a "barrel" is 42 US gallons).

The United States dominated world oil production for the first half of the twentieth century, accounting for over 50% of the world's annual production until 1960. After World War II demand for oil increased at a rapid rate and production increased fivefold between 1950 and 1972. As the world economy rapidly grew, international trade in oil was facilitated by the development of supertankers. The dominance of the United States decreased as several other regions increased their share of production, particularly the Middle East and the Soviet Union. The Organization of the Petroleum Exporting Countries (OPEC) was formed in 1960 and by 1972 was responsible for over 50% of the world's oil production. The cartel restricted the supply of oil during the 1970s, resulting in a fivefold increase in prices. The resulting fall in demand and oversupply led to a price collapse in the early 1980s. OPEC has subsequently never exceeded 42% of world production but the rapid economic expansion of many countries in the first decade of the twenty-first century resulted in relatively high prices again as demand increased substantially. Today 60% of the world's oil production is from six countries, of which five belong to OPEC.

Although natural gas had long been used in limited amounts for illumination, much of the natural gas that was originally discovered in association with oil was vented or flared because there was no way of commercializing the gas. Reliable pipelines to transport gas were not developed until after World War II. Natural gas is now used primarily for electrical generation in power plants, domestic heating, manufacturing fertilizers, and for other industrial purposes. World production of natural gas grew steadily in the 30 years after World War II, though at a slower rate than oil production. Production was dominated by the United States, which produced over 50% of the world's annual production until 1973. Since the early 1970s world gas production has risen at a similar rate to oil production. While the market for natural gas was once limited to the reach of pipelines, natural gas can now be transported globally using liquefied natural gas (LNG) tankers. This requires removal of impurities and cooling of the gas to approximately -160 C. LNG now accounts for 6% of the global market. Today ten countries produce 65% of the world's natural gas.

Together oil and natural gas currently comprise 54.3% of the world's total annual consumption of energy and, as such, are a major foundation of the global economy. In particular, the transportation of food, raw materials, and goods to market, as well as public and private transport systems, are all heavily dependent on oil and natural gas: they fuel over 96% of the transport sector. On the negative side they are a major source of CO2 emissions, though cleaner than coal per unit of power generated. The successful development of cleaner and economically viable alternative fuels is essential in the long run but the world's economy today is heavily dependent on the supply of oil and natural gas. This raises the question as to how much oil and natural gas remain in the ground. How long will oil and gas resources be available for mankind? [1]

Oil had been known since antiquity but it was not until the middle of the nineteenth century that wells were drilled for it, especially in Pennsylvania and on the shores of the Caspian. At first, it was primarily used as a fuel for lamps, replacing whale oil that was becoming scarce from overwhaling. That itself was a revolution for many people, adding an evening to the working day. The next step came in the 1860s when an enterprising German engineer, by the name of Nicholas Otto, found a way to insert the fuel directly into the cylinder of a steam engine, perfecting what became known as the *Internal Combustion Engine*, which was much more efficient. At first, it used benzene distilled from coal, before turning to petroleum refined from crude oil. The oil industry was

(*)Ripudaman Malhotra oil. Fossil Energy. Springer Science+Business Media New York 2013. P 8: 10

11

born. The first automobile took to the roads in 1882, changing the world in previously unimaginable ways. [1]

In order to understand how our global civilization came to be dependent on a finite source of energy, we need to know something about its formation and development as a resource. Although the sources of the organic material and the processes differ, all fossil fuels were formed from organic, carbon-based, life forms millions of years ago. This sequestering of carbon energy resources—oil, natural gas, and coal— helped provide us with the amicable climate that we have enjoyed up to the industrial revolution. Furthermore, all fossil fuels are finite natural resources subject to decline, which means that extraction follows the initial discovery and ends when the resources are exhausted.

---

[1] C.J. Campbell: Campbell's Atlas of Oil and Gas Depletion. Colin J. Campbell and Alexander Wöstmann 2013. P 3

1. What Is Energy?

Defining energy turns out to be more difficult than what one might think. The high school physics definition of energy "The ability to do work" does not take us very far, for what is ability? And what is work? What is the stuff (or non-stuff) that allows this to occur? Robert Romer wrote a good physics textbook which was about using energy concepts to understand all the conventional material of physics because "all physics is about energy." Yet even he admitted that he was unable to give a satisfactory definition of energy. He said we can see energy's effects, we can measure them, but we do not really know what it is.

Physicist Jacques Treiner recognizes the difficulty in defining energy precisely. He says "Energy, in the scientific context we are dealing with, is an abstract notion, of mathematical nature, which allows us to quantify the transformations of matter." Usually we detect energy containing or transforming materials (food or petroleum and oxygen) and energy being used because something is moved: a car, a basketball player, chemicals against a gradient, and so on. Hence energy can be thought of, not quite precisely, as that which causes motion. For our day-to-day experiences, energy is mostly found associated with either photons coming from the sun or the oxidation of fuels such as wood or food or oil that generates work (i.e., moves something) at some point in space and time. These are things we can experience and understand pretty well, even if the physicists cannot define them exactly, at least in a way that most of us can readily grasp. One of the things that makes energy easy for me to understand fairly well is that, having measured biological energy a great deal, I am impressed with the general sense and repeatability of the measurements. But I understand that I am not measuring energy itself, but rather its effects.

On a broader scale energy, or more precisely the transformations energy makes in matter, runs the world, figuratively and literally. Its effects are pervasive, relentless, and all-encompassing. While one cannot see energy, we can readily see its effects in transforming matter. What does this mean? It means we can readily and frequently observe the effects of energy transforming matter: you will your feet to go up the stairs and they do, lifting your body mass and generating heat. Your puppy shows incredible energy on a walk. Plants grow in sunshine and pretty much disappear when burned, meanwhile emitting light and heat. We can drop a stone from the top of a tower and watch it fall. We can step on the gas and a massive chunk of iron will be accelerated rapidly. Thus, we mostly do not observe energy directly but rather examine the effects of energy in transforming matter. Most of the energy around us is bound up in some kind of matter, contained in elevated rocks or water, the chemical bonds of wood or coal or food, warmer spaces inside our homes or other buildings, and so on. And we can readily observe bound energy being transformed into motion by watching cars zoom down the highway.

Physicist Jacques Treiner has thought a lot about energy. He says we do not live on energy. We live on transforming matter around us (and, C.H. adds, extracting the energy within it). One way of visualizing the notion is to ask how much matter has to be processed in order to deliver or consume a given amount of energy? The answer depends of course on the type of energy and the interactions involved in the process. The more intense the energy interaction involved, the less matter will be necessary.

For example, an energy transaction of 1 kWh (equivalent to 3.6 MJ) corresponds to (approximately): [1]

• 10 tons of water running down a medium-sized hydroelectric plant.

• The combustion of 1 kg of fossil fuel.

• The fission of 1 mg of uranium in a nuclear plant.

[1] Charles A.S. Hall: Energy Return on Investment. 2017. P 23:24

- The fusion of 5 lg of hydrogen in the center of Sun.

Obviously nuclear changes are much more intense than what we are used to. Coming back to the simple definition of energy as "the ability to do work" still seems somewhat vague and inadequate, for what is work? Does this include heat (well, the molecules are moving faster)? Most simply, but imperfectly to the physicist, work occurs when "something is moved." Thus energy, whatever that is, applied to transforming matter, is what causes motion to occur. Energy is experienced by humans most often as photons (with its associated energy) flowing from the sun or byproducts of the energy associated with those photons. We can see the atmosphere respond to this energy input as summer cumulous clouds rise into the atmosphere. We can watch water slowly disappear from a bowl. We can watch plants in our garden grow day to day as some small part of this photon flux is captured by plants through photosynthesis and stored as reduced (i.e., hydrogen— and energy—rich) chemical bonds associated with carbon. Then we can watch animals grow as they eat plants or other animals built with the energy of the plant, as that energy is passed as electrons associated with hydrogen through food chains to an electron acceptor such as oxygen. Thus, we are able to use the energy in a hamburger by oxidizing the reduced matter of the plant and animal tissue therein which initially was obtained by grass (such as wheat) that captured and stored that energy from the photons, and then passed it as chemical bonds to the cow and then to us. Likewise, when we drive an automobile we are oxidizing oil that is constructed of high-energy chemical bonds originally made with energy captured from the sun by algae but then processed over some 100 million years of geological pressure cooking.

Although the energy associated with each of these processes may be measured in very different units, they are all interchangeable, and "boil down" to the ability to heat water. So, we can generalize that, according to the laws of thermodynamics, all forms of energy share the ability to be turned into heat. This gives all different types of energy a common yardstick by which they can be measured. [1]

Global growth in demand of energy linked with an extended dependence on fossil fuel as an energy resource has contributed to a substantial rise in the atmospheric levels of carbon dioxide (CO_2). To make conditions worse, this step-up has been giving no indications of slowing down. As of now, renewables provide us 13 % of our energy, which could rise to 30 % by 2030. However, the fact still remains that fossil fuels will continue to

[1] Charles A.S. Hall: Energy Return on Investment. 2017. P 24

serve as the primary source of energy in the coming decades. According to the International Energy Agency, there has been an estimation that energy demand may foresee a hike by 45 % between now and 2030, if no remedial actions are taken to harness it. As also reported by International Energy Agency's (IEA's) World Energy Outlook 2007, there will be a transformation of growth in energy related to CO_2 emissions by 2030 as proposed to a rising 57 %. With rising worry about the likely climate changes on account of assemblage of greenhouse gases (GHGs) in the atmosphere has led to multiple studies of the phenomenon, focused on inventories of emissions, climate change models and other physical processes. For slackening and ceasing emissions, transformational alterations will be required in the energy sector, both in the way the world generates and consumes energy.

Carbon capture and storage (CCS) is a technology that comprises capture of carbon from industrial and power plants and its storage which facilities its isolation from the atmosphere for a large period of time. The possible storage methods include storage in coal beds (which can't be mined), geological formations (including the likes of depleted oil and gas fields), and deep saline reservoirs. This storage of CO_2 that occurs is mentioned as Geo sequestration or geologic storage. The utilization of CO_2 for enhanced oil recovery (EOR) is an instance of geological storage or geo sequestration. There are other storage sites in addition to geo sequestration, for storing CO_2, for example, oceans where there is injection onto the deep seafloor or by the direct discharge into ocean water column, followed by the fixation of CO_2 by inorganic carbonates. As recently researched there is a greater potential for using forestry as a means to sequester carbon for reduction of growth of emissions from India. An early estimate had suggested that over a period of a decade, with strong afforestation programs, around 17 % of energy emissions could be offset.

Countries like China and India with high population are heavily dependent on coal for generation of energy, thereby reporting a substantial rise in the quantity of coal-fired plants being constructed. As concurred by the UNFCC meeting (Copenhagen, 2009), following a settlement at the global level, CCS must be viewed as a vital technology in the quest for achieving carbon level reductions at the global level. Special and conclusive efforts need to be made so as to motivate the placement and operation of CCS in the developing world. [1]

Energy is the capacity to do work; in the physics field, work is something resulting from the action of a force such as that of gravity. In Nature there are different types of energy: the

[1] V. Vishal • T.N. Singh: Geologic Carbon Sequestration. Springer International Publishing Switzerland 2016. P 3: 4

most classic case is solar energy and all that energies come from the universe in the form of cosmic rays, X-rays, gravitational waves, dark matter, etc. A system that produces energy can be represented from a kite that "floats" in the clouds by means of wind, or a wave of light is passing through a space. According to the energy conservation law, for example, one of the first laws of thermodynamics, the total energy of a system is conserved, although it can be transformed into another form. Two billiard balls can collide, for example, and energy transformations are involved with sound and heat at the contact point: this phenomenon is derived from energy conservation law after the collision. In few words, all forms of energy can be converted into another. This had already begun when the man (or woman) lit the first fire by burning wood with the transformation of the chemical energy of the molecules in the form of heat. The energy transfer is based on energy conservation.

Other examples, a battery that generates electrons from chemical reactions, a toaster, the automobile, and many others. The sound is a form of kinetic energy: it is caused from vibration of the air molecules described as mathematical models. This vibration energy is transformed into electrical pulses that can be interpreted from the human as sound wave. In some systems such as that for the production of nuclear energy, the atoms are involved in multiple processes: the atoms of the nuclear fuel are divided by releasing the creation of thermal energy which is capture as water vapor to drive a kinetic energy generator. Subsequently, a motor turns it into a current flow to provide power supply. Renewable energy (replenished naturally) is generated from natural sources such as sunlight, wind, rain, tides, and geothermal heat, which are renewable (that are replenished naturally). Alternative energy is a term used for an energy source that is an alternative to the use of fossil fuels with a low environmental impact. In the International System of units (SI), the unit of energy is the joule, named thanks to James Prescott Joule. It is a derived unit and matched to the energy expenditure (or work) by applying a force of one Newton for a distance of one meter. However, energy is also expressed in many other units that are not part of the SI, as ergs, calories, British Thermal Units, kilowatt hours, and kilocalories, they require a conversion factor when expressed in SI units. In classical mechanics, from a mathematical point of view, energy is a conserved quantity. The work, a form of energy, is a force over a given distance described by the following equation:

$$w = \int_C F ds$$

The Eq. tells us that the work is equal to the line integral of the force along a path C. In the energy field some terms are used: Hamiltonian and Lagrangian. The total energy of a system can be expressed by Hamiltonian by using motion equation of William Rowan Hamilton. Another energy-related concept is called Lagrange, from Joseph-Louis Lagrange. This formalism is mathematically more convenient than the Hamiltonian for non-conservative systems (such as friction systems). The Lagrange is defined as the kinetic energy minus the potential energy. [1]

- **Main Sources of Energy on Earth**

Three main sources of energy exist on Earth: solar, geophysical, and nuclear. In a sense nuclear is the most basic, for fusion processes operate the Sun and fission heats the Earth's interior. Nuclear and geophysical working together define the heating of the Earth's interior, which pushes the continents apart in "continental drift" and causes "hot spots" where there are volcanoes and earthquakes. Africa fits nicely against South America, as was obvious to me looking at a world map in the 7th grade, and indeed it was once lodged there. Huge sources of radioactively- formed heat cause upward movements of the Earth's magma (hot rock), often in the middle of the oceans, and push the

---
([1])Maurizio Di Paolo Emilio: Microelectronic Circuit Design for Energy Harvesting Systems. Springer International Publishing AG 2017. P 11: 12

adjacent lithosphere ("plates") away from the heat source. Iceland with its many volcanoes is the Northern limit of the mid-Atlantic rift. The movements of the plates cause different pieces of the Earth to move and often smash into each other, generating earthquakes and volcanoes along the way.

The results can be most impressive: the Himalayan Mountains, highest on Earth, were formed when India sailed across the equator and smashed into the rest of the Asian Continent. California was formed by at least three land masses crashing into what is now Nevada. If the plate moves downward, back into the Earth, it creates a "subduction zone" and this is often associated with volcanoes and earthquakes. The Pacific Ocean is surrounded by a "ring of fire" due to these collisions and subductions, which includes the frequent earthquakes and volcanoes, alive or dormant, that are found along the West Coasts of the Southern Andes Mountains and the United States, including Alaska, the Aleutians, Kamchatka in Eastern Russia, much of Japan, New Guinea and New Zealand. All of this was started by hot spots in the middle of the Pacific Ocean, fueled initially by radioactive activity deep in the Earth.

Sometimes plates drift over a hot spot, generating an Island chain. Hawaii is one such example, with the northwestern most islands the oldest and the big island the newest, with active volcanoes on its southern shoulder.

The second main source of energy is another type of geophysical, which includes the inertia remaining from the formation of the solar system, but also the tides generated from this movement (seen mostly in ocean tides, but also in slight deformations of the Earth's crust such as the "bulge" at the equator) and also the crustal movements mentioned above. The most obvious inertial components include the daily rotation of the Earth about its own axis and the annual revolving of the Earth about the Sun. We get seasons because the Earth's axis is tilted at 23.5° relative to the plane of its revolution about the Sun, so in summer in the respective hemispheres the poles are pointed much more directly at the Sun and hence each square meter gets a larger photon flux or input of energy. Because the Earth is slowing down due to tidal friction (at milliseconds per century, so don't worry), like a slowing top, it is wobbling slightly. These wobbles, as well as other cyclical shifts in the relation of the Earth to the Sun, occur at three distinct thousands of year cycles, are called Milankovitch cycles and are thought the principal cause of long term climate cycles, such as ice ages. The Earth has had something like 12 distinct ice ages in its long history, and the relative warmth we enjoy now is not the normal situation over geological time.

The Sun is the source of energy for most of what we see from day to day on Earth.

It warms the atmosphere, operates the hydrological cycle and allows and feeds life. Eventually essentially all of this high-quality input of photons is transferred—at each work step and each transformation—to low grade heat in accordance to the second law of thermodynamics. The heat is then reradiated back to space as low-grade heat, maintaining the Earth at a relatively constant temperature. When the Sun's energy strikes the Earth's surface that portion that is not reflected does many types of work on the Earth's surface. We can feel the effects in the heating of dark surfaces, but the largest amount of work that sunlight does on Earth is to evaporate water. This is because it takes a great deal of energy to transform water from a liquid to a gaseous phase. Wind and more generally weather is caused by the uneven heating of the Earth's surface by the Sun. At a larger scale, the Sun heats the Earth more at the equator than toward the poles because the incident radiation is more intense there because the land is perpendicular to the photon flux.

You can see this for yourself by holding your hand at an angle to the Sun's rays on a bright sunny day and then slowly moving your hand so that it is perpendicular to the rays. You can feel your hand get warmer because more photons are striking each square centimeter of your hand. Similarly, more photons strike the Earth in the vicinity of the equator, so that the equator tends to warm more than other portions of the Earth. In general, this heat tends to be moved North and South by the oceanic (e.g., Gulf Stream) and especially atmospheric systems. There is a very special mechanism and pattern for this which we examine next. [1]

Energy sources vary in the level and timing of possible flow, very much like the money gifts from your aunts and uncle. Even though the amount in various reservoirs may be exactly the same, our society relies upon the flow of energy that can be provided in a given year, not the overall amount in the ground. Unfortunately for us, the easy fossil fuel deposits that we drilled first are also the ones that provided the biggest flow. The Ghawar field in Saudi Arabia, the monster of all oil deposits, is like the first aunt on steroids. Discovered in 1948 and starting production in 1951, Ghawar has been providing 5 million barrels per day, year after year ever since. No other oil field comes close. [2]

The Alberta tar sands may contain more oil than Ghawar and all the other Saudi oil

---

[1] Charles A.S. Hall: Energy Return on Investment. 2017. P 33: 35

[2] Roger Boyd: Energy and the Financial System Springer Cham Heidelberg New York Dordrecht London 2013. P 29

fields combined, but it has taken decades just to get production to near 2 million barrels per day. Extraction of oil from these tar sands is a huge, phenomenally complex, and capital-intensive job. Even the optimists see this source growing to only 3.5 million barrels per day by 2025. The tar sands are a bit like Aunt 2, but even more so. Drilling in the deep ocean, and now even in the Arctic, is also very much like Aunt 2. You have to wait a long time to get the oil flowing and that flow is quite limited. Many of the other energy sources, such as nuclear, wind, and solar, also have limitations on the flow of energy that they can provide. During the construction phase no energy is provided but a lot of energy is used and a lot of money invested. When the system goes online, the energy flow is like an annuity through regular instalments. [1]

    If a resource becomes too expensive the market responds in two ways: consumers tend to shift to alternative resources (demand reduction); and producers seek additional supplies through enhanced exploration activities and innovative production methods, thus enabling production from previously inaccessible deposits. During this transition period, resource availability is temporarily constrained and resource prices are highly

---

[1] Roger Boyd: Energy and the Financial System Springer Cham Heidelberg New York Dordrecht London 2013. P 29: 30

volatile – a situation often interpreted as the sign of imminent resource scarcity. [1]

Moreover, technology change and improvements in knowledge push the frontier of exploitable resources towards deeper, more remote or lower concentration occurrences, making resources a dynamically evolving rather than a 'fixed' quantity.

The terms reserves, resources and occurrences are routinely used in the resource industry but there is no consensus on their exact meanings. Many countries and institutions have developed their own expressions and definitions, and different authors and institutions have different meanings for the same terms. This lack of consistent definitions and boundaries is one cause of confusion. Another is rooted in the fact that most resource quantities, estimated as deposits, are often located several kilometers below the surface. The estimates are based on inherently limited information and the geological data derived from exploration activities are subject to interpretation and judgment. [2]

'resources' are defined as 'concentrations of naturally occurring solid,

---

[1] Ferenc L. Toth: Energy for Development Springer Science+Business Media Dordrecht 2012. P 150
[2] Ferenc L. Toth: Energy for Development Springer Science+Business Media Dordrecht 2012. P 151

liquid or gaseous material in or on the Earth's crust in such form that economic extraction is potentially feasible'. The geological dimension is divided into 'identified' and 'undiscovered' resources. 'Identified' resources are deposits whose location, grade, quality and quantity are known, or can be estimated from geological evidence. Identified resources are further subdivided into 'demonstrated' and 'inferred' resources, to reflect varying degrees of geological assurance, or lack thereof. 'Undiscovered' resources are quantities expected or postulated to exist based on materials found in analogous geological conditions. 'Other occurrences' are materials that are too low grade or for other reasons not considered technically or economically extractable. For the most part, unconventional resources are included in this category.

The boundary between 'reserves' and 'resources' is the current or expected profitability of exploitation, governed by the ratio of future market prices to the long-run cost of production. Price increases and production cost reductions expand reserves by moving resources into the reserve category and vice versa. Production costs of reserves are usually supported by actual production experience and feasibility analyses, while cost estimates for resources are often inferred from current production experience, adjusted for specific geological and geographical conditions. Reserve outlooks reported by the media are usually framed within a short-term market perspective, which focuses on prices, who is producing from which fields, where spare capacity might exist to meet short-term demand peaks, the politics of oil and how this all balances with demand. [1]

---

[1] Ferenc L. Toth: Energy for Development Springer Science+Business Media Dordrecht 2012. P 151: 152

2. What is hydrocarbons
2.1. Sources of Hydrocarbons

Three major types of hydrocarbons may be present in marine and coastal sedimentary environments: (1) petrogenic, which are generated in organic-rich source rocks exposed to elevated temperatures for long periods: a category that includes crude oil and its refined products; (2) biogenic, which are generated by biological processes or in the early stages of sediment diagenesis; and (3) pyrogenic (or pyrolitic) which are generated by combustion of fossil fuels.

Saturated (aliphatic) hydrocarbons comprise the majority of compounds in crude oils, typically 60–75 % by weight, followed by aromatic hydrocarbons. The former is by far the less toxic and display unique patterns associated with petroleum source, biogenic source (e.g. hydrocarbon inputs from plants), and degree of weathering. There are three types of saturated hydrocarbons in petroleum: normal alkanes (n-alkanes), branched alkanes (isoalkanes), and cyclic alkanes. The normal and branched alkanes are usually present in about equal amounts. The cyclic alkanes often are the most abundant alkanes in crude oil. [1]

---

[1] Kirsten Heimann • Obulisamy Parthiba Karthikeyan Subramanian Senthilkannan Muthu: Biodegradation and Bioconversion of Hydrocarbons. Springer

Modern industrial society is built upon and ruled by petroleum hydrocarbons. At a global level, crude oil productions are estimated to be more than 12 million metric tons annually and about 1.7–8.8 million metric tons of oil are released into the aquatic environment and soil respectively per annum. About 90 % of this emission is directly related to human activities including deliberate illegal waste disposal. Petroleum is essential to the current global networked economy, without it, our economic order would cease to function, bringing disaster to many populations. Yet the blessings of hydrocarbons are mixed, there is a growing awareness that imperfect petroleum technologies are changing ecosystems in ways that decrease the ability of these systems to support human populations. Effects of crude oil pollution in the environment will change from one source to another because of crude oil and its derivatives or mixture of organic compounds. Fuel oil may enter the water or soil environment as a result of spillages during transportation and by leakages from the storage facilities or pipelines. The more volatile components of fuel oils (low molecular weight alkanes) can be degraded in both water and soil and could volatize to enter into the atmosphere where they will form contaminants. The removal of contaminants from the environment is a crucial approach towards returning any environmental medium to its

Science+Business Media Singapore 2017. P 8: 9

natural/original state; hence the term "environmental restoration". While the introduction of contaminants or pollution of air, water and soil can be easy, rapid and persistent, the removal is often a daunting task. Remediation of petroleum-contaminated systems can be achieved by physical, chemical or biological methods. However, the unintended negative consequences of physical and chemical approaches are currently directing greater attention to the use of the biological alternatives. Therefore, the potential of remediation techniques will depend on the area where the spill has accrued among other factors. Oil spills in the water environment may affect microorganisms physically or induce direct toxicity. Hence, this chapter is designed to elucidate biological treatments, especially phytoremediation potential, as a green clean up technique for the restoration of the environment. [1]

Several conditions must be satisfied for a hydrocarbon accumulation to be established as a petroleum reservoir. The first is a sedimentary basin where a suitable sequence of rocks has accumulated over geological time. Within this sequence there must be a high content of organic matter, the source rock. The

[1] Kirsten Heimann • Obulisamy Parthiba Karthikeyan Subramanian Senthilkannan Muthu: Biodegradation and Bioconversion of Hydrocarbons. Springer Science+Business Media Singapore 2017. P 106

source rock reaches maturation through elevated pressure and temperature, a condition at which hydrocarbons are expelled through a process called migration and transferred into a porous type of sediment, the reservoir rock. Only if the reservoir is deformed in a favorable shape or if it is laterally grading into an impermeable formation, does a trap for the migrating hydrocarbons exist. [1]

In petroleum geology, source rock refers to a rock where hydrocarbons are being generated from organic matter. About 90 % of all organic matter found in sediments is contained in *shale,* which is a fine-grained clastic sedimentary rock composed of mud that is a mix of flakes of clay minerals. Continuous sedimentation over a long period of time causes burial of organic matter. These organic deposits can be divided into three groups depending on its origin and the type of hydrocarbon it produces. It may originate from *algal remains* deposited under anoxic (lack of oxygen) conditions in deep lakes or ocean. They tend to generate waxy crude oils when submitted to thermal stress during deep burial. Another source rock may be formed from *marine planktonic* and bacterial remains preserved under anoxic conditions in marine environments.

---

[1]Patrick A. Narbel • Jan Petter Hansen Jan R. Lien: Energy Technologies and Economics. Springer International Publishing Switzerland 2014. P 72

Source rocks which are formed from terrestrial *plant material* that has been decomposed by bacteria and fungi under oxic or sub-oxic conditions. They tend to generate mostly gas and light oils when thermally cracked during deep burials. Most coals and coaly shales are this kind of source rock. [1]

2.2. The Formation of Fossil Fuels

Very special circumstances were required for the formation of fossil fuels that are so important to our modern life. Coal, oil, and gas are organic materials, that is, they are plant and animal remain composed mostly of reduced (i.e., hydrogen rich) carbon as is all life. As plant life evolved some 3 billion years ago a great deal of organic material was formed, most of which was oxidized relatively soon and turned back to carbon dioxide in the atmosphere, which is not an energy source but is available for new plant growth. Some very small part of this organic material found its way to anaerobic (meaning without oxygen) basins, such as deep lakes or marine areas for oil and gas, and hence accumulated as various deposits.

Chemically natural gas (methane) has four molecules of hydrogen per molecule of carbon, oil has about equal amounts, and coal is

---

[1] Patrick A. Narbel • Jan Petter Hansen Jan R. Lien: Energy Technologies and Economics. Springer International Publishing Switzerland 2014. P 72: 73

mostly carbon, although with small amounts of hydrogen and sulfur and trace amounts of many elements, including troublesome mercury and uranium. Thus, there is a progressive increase in CO_2 per unit of energy delivered from natural gas to oil to coal, with coal releasing almost double the CO_2 per heat unit relative to gas.

The creation of exploitable oil and gas fields has been quite rare in the geologic past. It happened mostly some 90 and 150 million years ago when the Earth was very warm, and in very special and limited environments. The time required to turn the organic source material into oil and gas is extremely long and requires the organic material being buried at just the right depth (about 3000 m or two miles) and temperature (about 100 °C) to "pressure cook" the organic material into oil. As a consequence, significant quantities of commercially exploitable oil and gas are found in only a relatively few regions of the Earth's surface. Coal, formed in great fresh water swamps, required far less stringent conditions for its production and is more common. Gas too is widely dispersed, but large reservoirs are relatively rare. On the other hand, gas is found widely at low concentrations associated with coal and in "tight" shales and sandstones. Exploitation of these diffuse resources is becoming increasingly important as the large gas fields found earlier face serious depletion. Whether or not these newer "unconventional" fields can maintain production at the present level for very long is unknown at this time. [1]

In this developing world, where the coal reserves are still far greater when compared to oil and gas and hence, on an average 2 coal-based power stations are being constructed in a week, fossil fuels will continue to serve as a primary energy source for major parts of the world for this century.

As demonstrated in Fig. by International Energy Agency (IEA), fossil fuels fulfill more than 80 % of the primary energy needs; remaining portions are made up of atomic- and hydro-electricity, and renewable energy (like wind and solar energy, geothermal energy and biomass). Countries like United Kingdom which are having nuclear power and renewable energy sources also have large coal deposits. These deposits might serve as a suitable security in the future as an energy source. [2]

---

[1] Charles A.S. Hall: Energy Return on Investment. 2017. P 40: 41

[2] V. Vishal • T.N. Singh: Geologic Carbon Sequestration. Springer International Publishing Switzerland 2016. P 4: 5

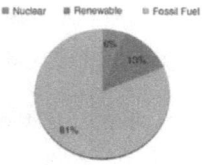

Fossil fuels originate from terrigenous and aquatic plants and animals deposited and preserved in oxygen-limited and/or acidic environments then buried so that the organic matter is not oxidized and returned to the biosphere as CO2. Coals usually come from woody plants deposited in swamps and bogs, while petroleum comes primarily from phytoplankton deposited in lakes and on continental shelves.

However, what is usually true is not always true. Boghead coals are derived from algae, and some oil and gas come from coals and terrigenous organic matter in organic-rich shale. Bitumen are fluid or fusible organic deposits that are soluble in organic solvents (or once were, as will be discussed later in greater detail), and crude oil is a special form of bitumen that can be produced through a pipe, although some restrict bitumen to mean a very heavy crude oil. This book will use the term primarily in the latter context.

Coal is a readily combustible rock containing more than 50 % by weight and 70 % by volume of fossil organic matter. Coals are subdivided into humic and sapropelic types.

Humic coals are by far the most abundant (*80 % of total) and are the type that come from woody plants. They are relatively high in oxygen content, at least initially, and low in hydrogen content. The United States has the largest humic coal deposits. Sapropelic coals (<10 % of total) come from spores, pollen, and algae and have much less oxygen and much more hydrogen. Boghead coals come primarily from algae, such as Botryococcus braunii. Cannel coals have high concentrations of spores. Sapropelic coals are more common in Australia and Asia, but boghead and cannel coals are still rare compared to humic coals, so the term coal ordinarily refers to humic coals.

Most sedimentary rocks contain disseminated organic matter (OM). This OM is usually distinguished as either kerogen or bitumen. Kerogen is the principal type, and it is defined as being insoluble in non-oxidizing acids, bases, and organic solvents. Some of the original sedimentary OM that is converted primarily to kerogen remains as, or is converted to be, soluble in organic solvents (i.e., bitumen sensu geochemists).

Kerogen can be derived from a variety of organic sources, and the source is reflected in the elemental composition. Sapropelic kerogens have higher hydrogen content from plankton, algae, and blue-green bacteria (also called blue-green algae, so I will not make the bacterial distinction henceforth). Humic kerogens have more oxygen and less hydrogen, consistent with their primary source being lignin from woody plants.

As organic matter is buried, it continues to evolve in composition, and sometimes oil and gas are expelled from the original deposit (i.e., source rock) and migrate to a reservoir. Historically, most oil and gas were produced from reservoir rocks, which can be porous sandstone or carbonate rock. Sapropelic source rocks generate primarily crude oil, although mature source rocks can also generate commercial quantities of natural gas. Coals and humic kerogens expel primarily gas during maturation, but some deposits of oil can be traced to humic coals and kerogens that contain significant amounts of algae and spores or waxy coatings on higher plant laves.

The insoluble organic matter left in the coal or source rock as it matures becomes more carbon-rich. For coal, increasing carbon content corresponds to an increase in rank, i.e., the progression from peat to lignite to bituminous to anthracite coals. For kerogen in petroleum source rocks, the classification is commonly a progression from immature (has not yet generated oil) to mature (is in the process of generating oil) to post-mature (all oil potential is exhausted).

Although crude oil is technically a form of bitumen, the term bitumen is more commonly synonymous with asphalt, meaning a highly viscous to semi-solid or even solid amorphous material. This usage of the term can apply to materials that were expelled or extruded from a rich source rock at low maturity (e.g., asphalt seeps along the coast of southern California; gilsonite dikes in Utah) or resulted from changes after migration to a reservoir (e.g., extra heavy crude oils in Athabasca, Canada, and Orinoco, Venezuela). To avoid confusion, this document will refer to naturally occurring semi-solid to solid bitumen as asphaltic bitumen.

Asphaltic bitumen can be precipitated in a reservoir by solubility changes related to temperature and pressure or increased light oil content or can be the residue of degradation caused by water washing, seepage of light hydrocarbons through the cap rock, bacterial action, or some combination of all three.

Sometimes bitumen is exposed over geologic time to temperatures high enough for it to continue to mature, i.e., continue to become more carbonaceous as hydrogen-rich moieties are split off and escape. At some point corresponding approximately to the transition from mature to post-mature kerogen or bituminous to semi-anthracite coal, the bitumen becomes insoluble and is thereafter called pyrobitumen. Unfortunately, the term pyrobitumen is often used in oil shale retorting literature to denote early, heavy pyrolysis products of kerogen, as will be described later.

Oil shale is merely a rich, sapropelic, petroleum source rock that has not been buried deeply enough to form oil and gas. The definition is more technological than scientific. The historical definition of oil shale was that it was shallow enough that it could be mined and retorted in a surface facility, although in situ forms of retorting have expanded the definition. This definition implies that the organic content is high enough that mining (or drilling) and retorting can be accomplished with net energy and economic gain, or that it is conceivable that it will be in the future. That cutoff is somewhere in the range of 5–10 wt% of oil yield. The term kerogen (derived from the Latin for "wax generator") originally described the organic matter in Scottish oil shale (torbanite), but its modern usage is for all disseminated insoluble organic matter. [1]

---

[1] Alan K. Burnham: Global Chemical Kinetics of Fossil Fuels. Springer International Publishing AG 2017. P 2: 4

2.3. Earth's Carbon Inventory: Its Origin and Abundance

2.3.1. Earth's Major Carbon Reservoirs

Carbon is the backbone of life on the Earth and, possibly, in the Universe. (According to the *Carbon Chauvinism* hypothesis, due to the unique chemical properties of carbon, life can only exist on the planets where it could be evolved from carbon based structural units.) Carbon's unique capacity for forming multiple bonds and long-chain molecules (biopolymers) makes life possible; carbon comprises about half the dry weight of most living organisms. Starting from the discovery of fire, our civilization vitally depends on carbon for its livelihood. Carbon-based fossil fuels powered the Industrial Revolution and brought about the rise in the standard of living we currently enjoy. Almost everything we get energy from, whether through

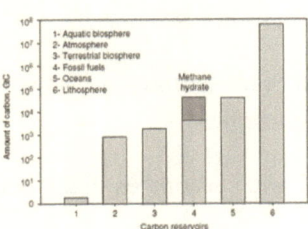

food (carbohydrates) or through fuels at power stations (gas, coal) and transport (gasoline, jet, and diesel fuels), is based on one form of carbon-based compounds or another.

For this very reason, our civilization is rightfully called *"Carbon Civilization."*

Carbon's abundance on our planet is surprisingly low: the lithosphere has only 0.032 wt.% of carbon in all its forms (for comparison, iron's abundance is 5 wt.%).

Over geologic timescale, most of the carbon on the Earth became locked up in sedimentary rocks as carbonates and fossil fuels, and significant part of it got dissolved into the oceans as CO_2, carbonate (CO_3^{2-}), and bicarbonate (HCO_3^-) ions.

Available data show that the atmospheric CO_2 concentration gradually reached the level of about 0.02–0.03 vol.% and fluctuated within this range for about half a million years.

Carbon is stored on our planet in the following major carbon reservoirs:

• Carbonates and other sedimentary rock deposits in the lithosphere

• Dissolved CO_2 and carbonates in the ocean

• Soil organic matter

• Fossil fuel deposits

• Living and dead organisms in the biosphere

• CO_2 in the atmosphere

The Figure depicts the relative abundance of the major carbon reservoirs on the Earth.

Inorganic deposits of carbon in the lithosphere in the form of limestone, dolomite, chalk, and other carbonates (representing the most thermodynamically stable form of carbon) constitute the largest reservoir of carbon on our planet.

Organic forms of carbon, e.g., carbon in biosphere (plants, living organisms) and soil organic matter (e.g., humus), represent significantly lesser share of the total carbon inventory compared to inorganic forms of carbon. The amount of carbon in the form of carbon-bearing fossil fuels, i.e., coal, oil, natural gas (NG), peat, tar, and bitumen, is estimated at about 5,000 Gt, however, if the potentially recoverable resources of methane hydrates would be factored in this figure would increase by almost one order of magnitude (Gt is gigaton or 10^9 ton). [1]

---

[1] Nazim Muradov: Liberating Energy from Carbon: Introduction to Decarbonization. Springer Science+Business Media New York 2014. P 1: 3

2.3.2. Origin of Carbon Fuels: Biotic vs. Abiotic

It is widely recognized that the occurrence of CO_2 in the early atmosphere and near surface environment was the result of degassing of the Earth's interior: as its surface cooled, the volcanoes released massive amounts of CO_2, steam (H_2O), ammonia (NH_3), and methane (CH_4). The early primitive life forms started photosynthesizing food, energy, and oxygen (O_2) using sunlight, CO_2, and water:

$$CO_2 + H_2O + \text{sunlight} \rightarrow (CH_2O) + O_2$$

where (CH_2O) refers to a photosynthesis product.

During this early evolution process, CO_2 concentration in the atmosphere was gradually reduced and the concentration of O_2— increased. Green plants further facilitated the conversion of CO_2 to O_2. Nitrogen (N_2) was built up in the atmosphere partly through the oxidation of NH_3 with O_2, but predominantly from denitrifying bacteria. Atmospheric methane concentration decreased via oxidative pathways (the reaction with O2). As O_2 levels increased in the atmosphere, the ozone layer was formed, which started to filter out harmful ultraviolet (UV) radiation. This facilitated the evolution of living organisms and species first in the shallow seas and later throughout the Earth. Buried under thick layers of rocks, the remains of marine organisms, swamp plants, and incompletely decayed plant matter exposed to high pressures and temperatures were transformed to fossil fuels: coal and hydrocarbons (liquid and gaseous), through an anaerobic decomposition process over the geological time scale of hundreds of millions of years (according to some estimates, about 650 million years). Because of a nonuniformity of the "feedstock" and different conditions of the transformation process, globally, no two coals or oils or gases have the same chemical composition.

According to this theory, from the historical perspectives, all types of carbon-bearing fuels, including biomass and fossil fuels, have been originated from solar-powered photosynthesis of a biological matter (that was eventually converted into different types of fuels as we know them today). These carbonaceous fuels are differentiated based on the timescale required for their formation: from million to hundred million years for coal and hydrocarbons (oil and gas), and from hundreds to thousands of years for peat, and from days to hundreds of years for biomass. On the scale of human lifespan, coal, oil, and gas are defined as *fossil* or *nonrenewable* fuels, whereas biomass and associated biofuels as *renewable* fuels. It should be noted, however, that this classification is arbitrary: for example, peat is considered fossil fuel, although in terms of its formation timescale it overlaps with biomass.

There are, however, competing theories of the carbon fuels origin on the Earth; for example, one of them infers that carbon first arrived on our planet in a reduced form, as found in almost all meteorites, and it was *abiotic* (or *abiogenic*) in origin. The supporters of this theory hypothesize that an early ocean contained a high concentration of photochemically produced complex organic compounds formed under reducing conditions, which led to the formation of a reduced carbon reservoir near Earth's surface. The oxidation of subducted organic rich sediments during upper-mantle magma genesis slowly released CO_2 to the surface environment on a timescale consistent with the rate of oxygenation of the surface environment by photosynthetic cyanobacteria, with the record of carbon isotopes in sedimentary rocks and with the record of carbonate sedimentation. One of the strengths of this hypothesis is that the proposed "reduced carbon reservoir" is a more favorable environment for the emergence of life (compared to an oxidized carbon route via CO_2). This model also provides a suitable explanation of the early methane-enhanced greenhouse effect.

According to other (older) abiotic hypothesis, fossil fuels (e.g., oil) were formed from deep carbon deposits, most likely, during the formation of the Earth. This hypothesis suggests that petroleum originated from carbon-bearing fluids that migrated upward from the mantle, which implies that more oil could exist on our planet than previously estimated. The presence of methane on other planets, e.g., Jupiter, Saturn, Uranus, and Neptune, supports this theory, since this fact is cited as an evidence of the formation of hydrocarbons without the involvement of biological processes. Lately, this theory fell out of favor because it failed to make any useful prediction for the discovery of large oil deposits. However, the abiotic theory still has many supporters, and it cannot be dismissed because the mainstream theory of fossil fuels origin still has to be established conclusively. [1]

2.4. Hydrocarbon Systems (Saudi Arabia as an example)

The hydrocarbon province of central and eastern Saudi Arabia constitutes two major petroleum systems; the Paleozoic and Jurassic petroleum systems. Each system includes regionally extensive source rock facies and multi reservoirs and seals pairs. A relatively minor hydrocarbon system exists in the Triassic lower Jilh Formation.

(¹)Nazim Muradov: Liberating Energy from Carbon: Introduction to Decarbonization. Springer Science+Business Media New York 2014. P 3: 4

Geochemical studies concluded that that the Paleozoic System was sourced primarily from the "hot" shale in the basal Qusaiba Member of the Silurian Qaliba Formation. Basin modeling indicates that the Qusaiba "hot" shale has been generating hydrocarbons since the mid-Cretaceous time. Gas generation from the Qusaiba "hot" shale, which started in the Cretaceous, dominates in eastern Saudi Arabia whereas oil generation is in relatively small areas in central Saudi Arabia. Main reservoirs in the Paleozoic system exist in the sequence above the source rock, specifically in the Khuff, Unayzah, and Jauf Formations.

The regional seal of the Paleozoic system is the Triassic Sudair shale, which completely separates it from the overlying Mesozoic systems. The Silurian Qusaiba "hot" shale forms the main source and ultimate seal to the secondary sub-Qusaiba reservoirs in the Silurian Sarah Formation.

The prolific Jurassic oil system of Saudi Arabia constitutes two organic-rich intervals of carbonate mudstones in the Tuwaiq and Hanifa Formations as source rocks. Porous carbonate facies forming reservoir units along with anhydrites or argillaceous carbonates forming sealing units exist in the Dhruma, Tuwaiq, Hanifa, Arab, and Hith Formations. The Jurassic reservoirs constitute the main oil producing units in Saudi Arabia. Oil reservoirs also exist in the Cretaceous and Tertiary Formations, and they are charged mainly from the Jurassic source rocks. [1]

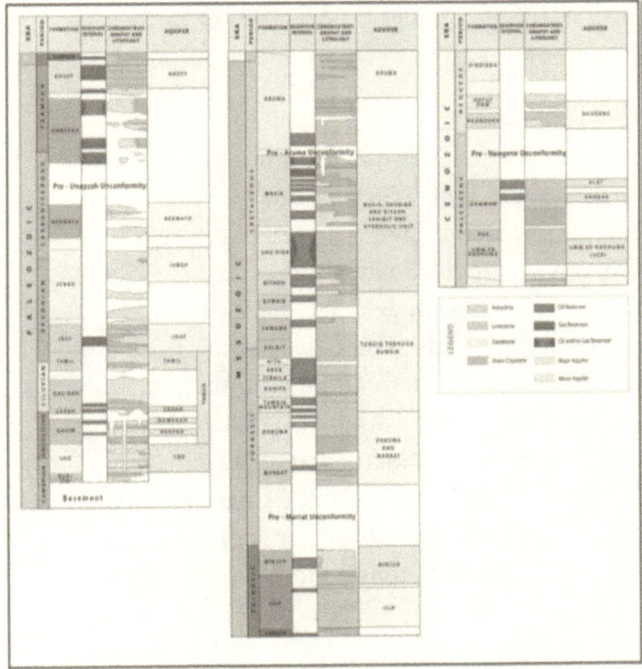

Based on generalized plate-scale chrono stratigraphy charts, unconformities, sea level variation, climate and the paleogeographic location of the plate across geological times, the impacts of paleoclimate and tectonic activity on

[1] François Roure • Ammar A. Amin Sami Khomsi • Mansour A.M. Al Garni: Lithosphere Dynamics and Sedimentary Basins of the Arabian Plate and Surrounding Areas. Springer International Publishing AG 2017. P 39: 40

depositional environments and hydrocarbon evolution can be highlighted.

The Paleozoic rock series have been characterized, accordingly, through two distinct cycles.

During an early Paleozoic cycle (Cambrian—Ordovician— Silurian), the Arabian plate was first located near the equatorial line in the Cambrian time, resulting in a relatively warmer climate, and an increase in the accommodation space due to induced sea level variation. This coincided with rifting, extension, at the northern Gondwana margin. In the Ordovician, the Arabian plate drifted towards the south latitudes and that coincided with several tectonic pulses. Consequently, collision tectonics led to major uplifts (e.g., Oman), and affected considerably sedimentary and facies patterns. The Arabian plate continuously moved toward the South Pole until it reached the latitude of 55°. Here, the paleoclimate witnessed an expansion of major continental ice sheets in Ashgillian time, and the effects of late Ordovician

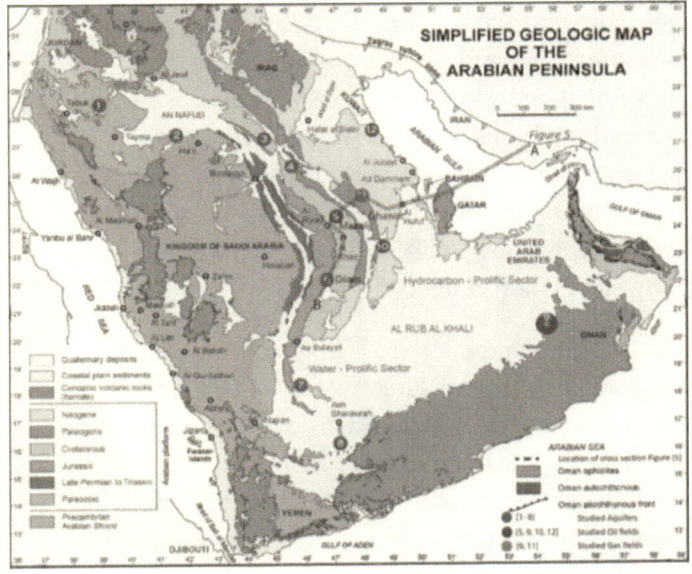

glaciations, which reached eastward, from Jordan through western Saudi Arabia. This remained until the Silurian, when the whole plate returned to

the equatorial line. It was accompanied with the increase in temperature, resulting in deglaciation and sea level rise, consequently source rock (hot shale) deposited in anoxic conditions.

The late Paleozoic cycle (Carboniferous—Permian— Early Triassic), started with a remarkable event of erosion and non-deposition driven by the propagation of far field compressional stresses through the area, the "Hercynian event". The Arabian plate moved again toward the South Pole and the paleoclimate started to control the plate-scale depositional processes. Glaciations spanned the Late Carboniferous and ended with return to the equatorial line associated with increased temperatures in the late Permian— early Triassic, coincident with slab pull in the south-facing subduction zone.

Throughout the Mesozoic, the stratigraphic architectures and geometries confined within the Arab Basin, resulted from the sea level fluctuations, due to the effects of eustatic changes or relative uplift and subsidence in the vicinity of the Arabian Arch. Besides, the petroleum systems within this Basin (and the hydrocarbon—prolific sector) are pretty much influenced by such stratigraphic configuration. During the middle Jurassic to early Cretaceous times, the axial zone of the Arabian plate underwent subsidence in both prolific and non-prolific sectors, leading to sea level rise and marine sedimentation covering large areas of the Arabian plate.

Economics of Petroleum, Principles

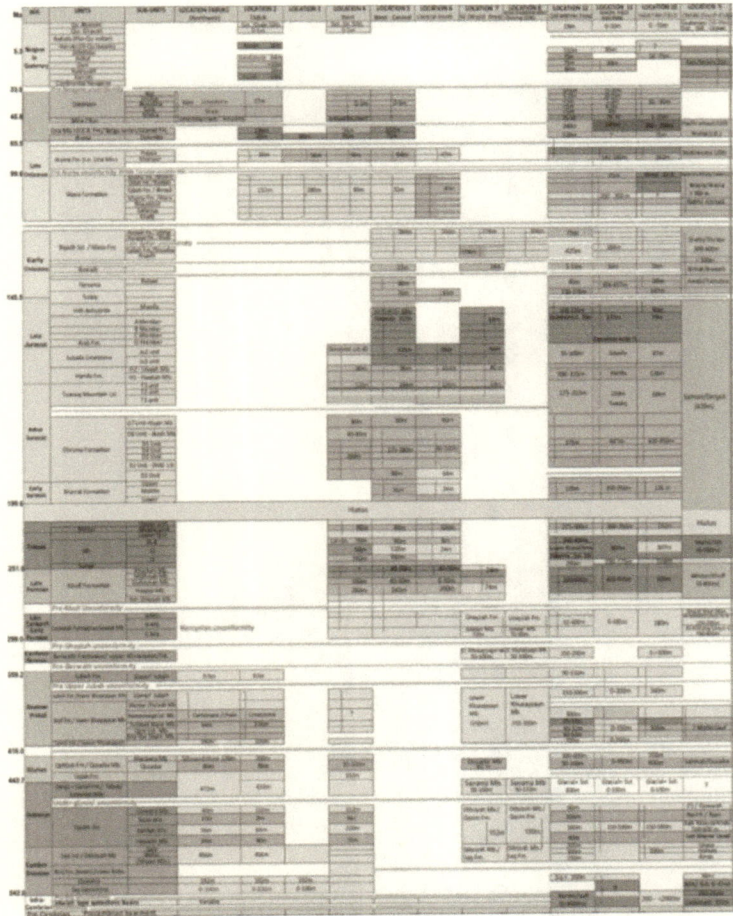

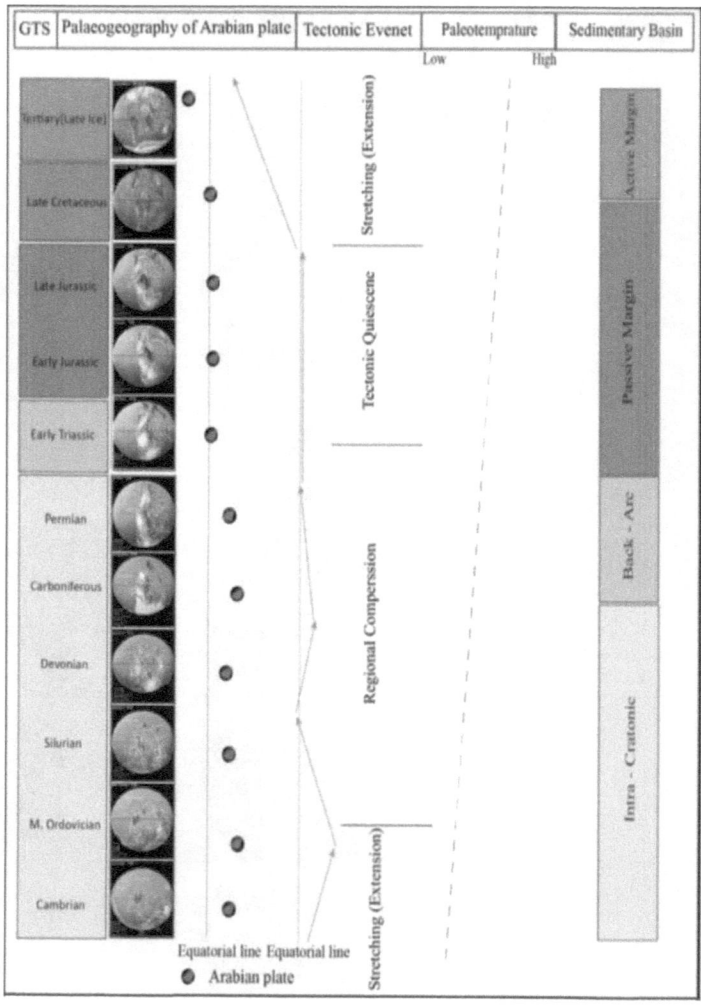

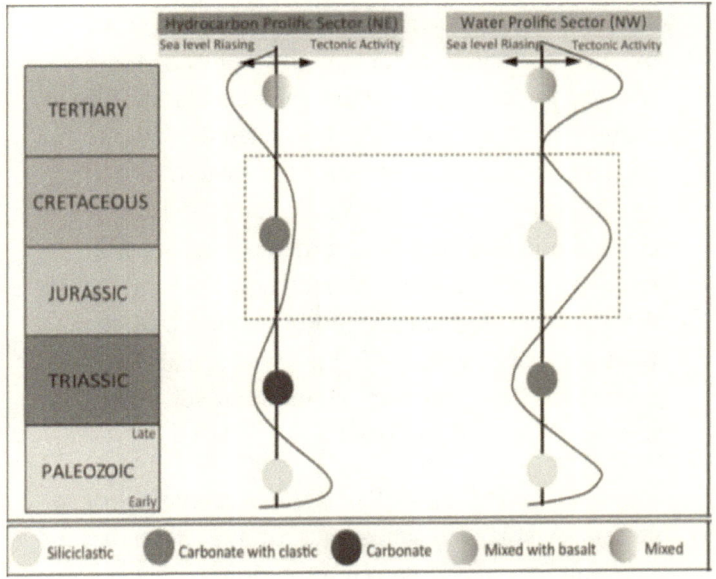

From early to middle Cretaceous, continuous subsidence in the Arabian arch occurred in the hydrocarbon-prolific sector, whereas the Arabian Arch was reactivated and uplifted towards the west in the non-prolific sector. This led to a local sea level fall and deposition of siliciclastic (marine and non-marine series).

Accordingly, there are obvious differences in the tectonic evolution between prolific and non-prolific areas, which could be illustrated through the presence of distinct structural features. In the prolific area (eastern margin of the Arabian Gulf), there are wide spreading of faults due to extension and subsidence, whereas in the western part, uplift structure is dominant and that can be observed by the difference in topography between these two areas. In addition, the thicknesses of the sediments may reflect the related tectonic events, which increase toward the eastern part of Saudi Arabia, and that could be due to the continuing subsidence and deposition, mostly without breaks and evidenced by a decrease of the number of unconformities, whereas in the western part, most of the geological rock formations are thinner, with relatively high number of unconformities.

The major Paleozoic reservoirs of central Arabia are sandstones of the Devonian Jauf and Permian Unayzah formations.

Further to the east, in the Arabian Gulf region, the main Paleozoic reservoirs are made up of carbonates of the Upper Permian Khuff formation. Other reservoirs include clastics of pre-Qusaiba sequence that are fault-bounded and sourced laterally by down-faulted Qusaiba shale member.

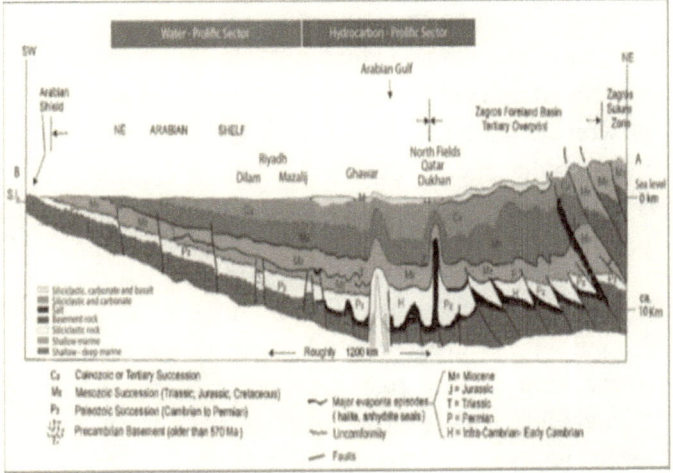

These reservoirs are characteristically affected by silica cementation, which decreases their flow properties.

Many of the Ordovician sandstone reservoirs are sealed by the overlying Lower Silurian Qusaiba shale. The Devonian Jauf sandstone reservoir is sealed by a very distinctive shaly unit called (D3B) in the Ghawar field.

The impermeable anhydrite, carbonate rocks and shale beds of the Khuff formation and/or equivalent unit, also constitute a major regional seal for the central Arabia, Qusaibah Paleozoic sequence. Basal Khuff strata form the top seal to the Permian Unayzah reservoir in Ghawar field.

Traps are mostly structural and related to basement block faulting, tectonic salt movement and deformation (halokinesis) as well as wrench faulting. Generally, in Saudi Arabia and Iraq the direction of hydrocarbon migration is toward the west.

The best and most prolific Mesozoic reservoirs occur in the Upper Jurassic Arab formation; especially Arab C and D members, where bulk rock porosity averages 25 % and permeability exceeds 100 md. Seal units for the carbonate rock reservoirs of the major Arab formation are made up of anhydrite beds of the upper part of the Arab and Hith formations. Other known reservoirs include the porous carbonate-rock units within the Hanifa and Tuwaiq Mountain formations. During the middle Cretaceous, regressive sandstones, which are prolific hydrocarbon reservoirs (Wara, Safaniya, Khafji) of the Wasia group, were deposited. They are sealed by Rumailah member which consists of limestone, and Ahmadi member which consists of shale of the Wasia formation. [1]

---

[1] François Roure • Ammar A. Amin Sami Khomsi • Mansour A.M. Al Garni: Lithosphere Dynamics and Sedimentary Basins of the Arabian Plate and Surrounding Areas. Springer International Publishing AG 2017. P 52: 57

3. What Is Petroleum?

Petroleum and natural gas have similar origin and often occur together in geologic formations, and their global distribution and production is discussed together in the entry by McCabe. This entry makes clear the distinction between reserves and resources. Reserves represent only that fraction of the resource base that can be economically recovered using current technology. These are not fixed quantities as both technology and economics change over time. Global annual production (and consumption) of oil in 2010 was 31 billion barrels and of natural gas was around 120 trillion cubic feet. In energy units, they correspond to 180 EJ of oil and 120 EJ of natural gas. The current reserves are estimated at 1,236 billion barrels of conventional oil (7,500 EJ) and 6,545 tcf of natural gas (6,500 EJ). The current reserves to production ratio (R/P) is about 40 for oil and about 55 for natural gas. The R/P ratio has often been mistakenly taken as the time to exhaustion, but new discoveries as well as advances in technology add to the reserves. In the case of oil, for example, the R/P ratio has stayed around 40–50 years for more than 60 years even with the steadily increasing oil consumption. In addition, there are also unconventional accumulations of these hydrocarbon resources and extracting them requires development of new technologies. In the case of oil, the unconventional resources are oil sands, oil shale, and heavy oil. Unconventional resources of natural gas are coal bed methane, tight gas, shale gas, and gas hydrates. These unconventional resources are vast and have the potential of more than doubling our resource endowment.

Exploration and production of oil from sedimentary deposits and oil sands is the subject of an entry by Speight. The processes for recovering oil could be a simple matter of drilling into the formation with the oil flowing to the surface under its own pressure, or it may require injection of gases, fluids, and surfactants to coax it to flow. In extreme cases, it may even require underground combustion of a portion of the resource to release the oil. Speight describes the chemical and physical factors that govern the flow of oil and the technology options currently available. In a different entry, Speight provides and account of the different processes such as distillation, catalytic cracking, hydrotreating, reforming, and DE asphalting used in the refining of crude oil. This entry also deals with environmental effects of the gaseous, liquid, and solid effluents from these processes. Production of oil from shale is principally achieved by retorting of shale, or other thermal processes including in situ pyrolysis. Oja and Suuberg detail the chemistry and technology of these processes in the entry. [1]

Oil remains the prized fuel. It has a high energy density and as a liquid it is well suited for transportation. The transportation sector relies on oil for over 90% of its energy needs (the remainder being mostly furnished by coal – via electricity).

Given the importance of liquid fuels, there is considerable interest in converting coal and natural gas, the other hydrocarbon resources, into oil. In a pair of entries, Araso and Smith provide an overview of the various processes for converting natural gas and coal to liquids. These reviews cover the basic chemistry and catalytic technologies behind the different approaches. The entry on Gas to Liquid Technologies deals with steam reforming of methane, auto thermal reforming, and partial oxidation approaches for producing syngas, including strategies for managing the heat and mass transfer through the use of different reactor technologies. The entry next covers the conversion of syngas into liquids by Fischer-Tropsch (FT) synthesis. The entry on Coal to Liquids Technologies reviews the different approaches like pyrolysis, direct liquefaction, coprocessing with petroleum, and indirect liquefaction that first converts coal into syngas and then uses FT or other conversion processes to make liquid fuels. [1]

([1])Ripudaman Malhotra: Fossil Energy. Springer Science+Business Media New York 2013. P 2

([1])Ripudaman Malhotra: Fossil Energy. Springer

At the 11th World Petroleum Congress in 1983, the definition of petroleum is finally determined by three organizations: API, SPE, and AAPG. [1]

Petroleum is a mixture which is mainly composed of hydrocarbon compounds and exists naturally in gas, liquid, and solid in nature. It includes crude oil and natural gas. This is a broad definition of petroleum. Narrowly, petroleum is a flammable liquid or solid mineral mainly composed of a variety of hydrocarbons. Crude oil is the unprocessed liquid petroleum which is recovered from oil wells.

Petroleum is a thick, flammable, yellow-to-black mixture of gaseous, liquid, and solid hydrocarbons that occurs naturally beneath the Earth's surface, can be separated into fractions including natural gas, gasoline, naphtha, kerosene, fuel and lubricating oils, paraffin wax, and asphalt and is used as raw material for a wide variety of derivative products.

Petroleum is a dark-colored thick flammable crude oil occurring in sedimentary rocks around the Persian Gulf, in parts of North and South America, and below the North Sea, Science+Business Media New York 2013. P 3

([1])Xuetao Hu • Shuyong Hu Fayang Jin • Su Huang: Physics of petroleum Reservoirs, Petroleum Industry Press, Beijing, China 2017. P 166 consisting mainly of hydrocarbons. Fractional distillation separates the crude oil into petrol, paraffin, diesel oil, lubricating oil, etc. Fuel oil, paraffin wax, asphalt, and carbon black are extracted from the residue.

Petroleum [L. petroleum, from Greek: petra (rock) + Latin: oleum (oil)] or crude oil is a naturally occurring, flammable liquid consisting of a complex mixture of hydrocarbons of various molecular weights and other liquid organic compounds, that are found in geologic formations beneath the Earth's surface. Petroleum is recovered mostly through oil drilling. It is refined and separated, most easily by boiling point, into a large number of consumer products, from gasoline and kerosene to asphalt and chemical reagents used to make plastics and pharmaceuticals. [1]

In petroleum engineering, the reservoir engineer is primarily interested in the properties of crude oil. A detail description of physical properties of crude oil is necessary to the theoretical study and application of petroleum reservoir engineering in oil production.

The nature of crude oil changes greatly. It is dependent on the composition of the oil, namely the proportion of hydrocarbons and

---

[1] Xuetao Hu • Shuyong Hu Fayang Jin • Su Huang: Physics of petroleum Reservoirs, Petroleum Industry Press, Beijing, China 2017. P 166

nonhydrocarbons in the oil. Moreover, the properties of in-place oil are also different from those of oil at surface conditions owing to the great difference in temperature and pressure. In reservoirs, in-place oil often contains a great deal of dissolved gas. When produced to the surface, the in-place oil will shrink and become more viscous because of the release of dissolved gas from the oil. Therefore, there are many differences between in-place oil and the oil at the surface conditions. [1]

Hydrocarbons are the major constituent of crude oil pollution which persist in the environment for long periods due to their hydrophobic nature. In recent decades, environmental pollution due to petroleum and petrochemical products attracted more researchers to work in this area of research. Polycyclic aromatic hydrocarbons (PAHs) are ubiquitous with toxic, mutagenic and carcinogenic nature. The fate of PAHs in the environment is associated with both abiotic and biotic factors including volatilization, adsorption and microbial transformation. They are generated from both natural and anthropogenic processes, and pose a serious concern on the health of aquatic life and human beings through bioaccumulation. [2]

---

[1] Xuetao Hu • Shuyong Hu Fayang Jin • Su Huang: Physics of petroleum Reservoirs, Petroleum Industry Press, Beijing, China 2017. P 246

Most substances normally exist in three *phases*: the solid phase, the liquid phase and the gas phase. Temperature and pressure will decide in which phase a substance exists. Solids have a tendency to keep their shape and volume when subject to moderate external forces. Liquids on the other hand, will change their shape but retain their volume, and gas will change both shape and volume. Nevertheless, there is no clear separation between the three phases, especially not between liquid and gas, which is often denoted by the common name: *fluids*. Both oil and gas are therefore fluids.

At the same time, they belong to a chemical group called *hydrocarbons* because their molecules mostly consist of hydrogen and carbon atoms, but may also include Sulphur, nitrogen, oxygen and metallic compounds. We use the term *petroleum* about the mixture of hydrocarbons that we want to recover from a petroleum reservoir.

Depending on temperature and pressure, it may be a liquid, a gas or even a solid phase. The hydrocarbons found in a petroleum reservoir vary from the simple molecule *methane* (CH_4) with a molecule weight of 16, to naphthene and polycyclic molecules with a

---

[2]Kirsten Heimann • Obulisamy Parthiba Karthikeyan Subramanian Senthilkannan Muthu: Biodegradation and Bioconversion of Hydrocarbons. Springer Science+Business Media Singapore 2017. P 138

molecule weight of more than a thousand. All molecules have been created through thermal or bacterial decomposition of organic matter subject to high pressure and temperature during millions of years.

It is often more practical to refer to a special hydrocarbon by the number of carbon atoms in the molecule instead of the exact chemical formula. Methane is then denoted C_1, propane C_3 etc. The components which are liquids under atmospheric or *standard conditions* (1 atm $= 1.013 \times 10^5$ Pa and $T = 15$ °C) are described as *crude oil* in commercial contexts. Crude oil may consist of thousands of different molecule types and can vary from a light-brown liquid to a very high viscosity tar-like fluid. Crude oils are often broadly categorized by using properties which are easy to measure in the field, such as the gravity of the oil. For historical reasons the gravity is measured in *degrees API* (American Petroleum Institute) which is defined: [1]

$$°API = \frac{141.15}{\rho_0} - 131.5$$

---

[1] Patrick A. Narbel • Jan Petter Hansen Jan R. Lien: Energy Technologies and Economics. Springer International Publishing Switzerland 2014. P 71: 72

where $\rho 0$ is the density in g/cm3. Crude oil is then classified according to its density. Because of the high temperature and pressure in a petroleum reservoir, the oil usually contains dissolved gas. When the oil is brought to the surface some of the gas will be released, which results in a shrinkage of the oil volume. The gas/oil ratio (GOR) is a dimensionless number equal to the ratio of the released gas volume to the oil volume at the surface (at standard conditions). The GOR and the API is a first indication of the quality of the oil.

3.1. source and reservoir rocks

Hydrocarbons are found in porous and permeable rocks, usually sandstones and limestones, in close proximity to source rocks, usually shales, that have an abundance of organic material. This material has been converted over millions of years to oil and gas under the intense pressure and high temperature encountered deep in the earth.

Reservoir rocks must have void spaces in which fluids can be stored, and the void spaces must be interconnected in order for fluids to move through the rocks. Porosity is a measure of the amount of void space compared to the total volume of the rock. Permeability is a measure of the flow property of the rocks, and is given in a unit called a millidarcy. A typical sand reservoir, such as the Woodbine sand in the

East Texas field, has average porosity of 25% and permeability of 1500 millidarcy. A rock with permeability of 5 millidarcy or less is considered a tight formation. [1]

The third factor necessary for hydrocarbon accumulation is a trapping mechanism. If for no other reason than the force of gravity, gas, oil, and water in a closed container will separate because of differences in their specific gravities, gas will rise to the top, and water will settle at the bottom, with oil forming an intermediate layer. So, it happens in the earth. Over millions of years, the hydrocarbons will migrate to the highest point within the reservoir rock. If the reservoir rock is wrinkled, the hydrocarbons will mi- grate to the top of the wrinkle; if the reservoir rock is faulted, they will migrate to the face of the fault; if the reservoir rock is truncated or pinched out up dip, they will migrate to the termination of the reservoir rocks; if the reservoir rock abuts up dip against an impervious barrier such as a salt dome, they will migrate to the flanks of the dome, but they will accumulate at these location only if an impervious barrier exists above to create a trap. If no such impervious barrier exists, the hydrocarbons will continue to migrate until they accumulate somewhere where a trap does exist. [2]

---

[1] R.L.Sengbush: petroleum exploration, a quantitative introduction, library of congress 1st edition 1986. p 9

Reservoir rocks are either of *clastic* or *carbonate* composition. Both are sedimentary rocks. The former is composed of silicates, usually sandstone, the latter of biogenetically derived detritus, such as coral or shell fragments. There are some important differences between the two rock types which affect the quality of the reservoir and its interaction with fluids which flow through them.

The main components of sandstone reservoirs (siliciclastic reservoirs) is quartz (SiO_2). Chemically it is a fairly stable mineral which is not easily altered by changes in pressure, temperature or acidity of pore fluids. Sandstone reservoirs form after the sand grains have been transported over long distances e.g. by rivers or wind, and have been deposited in particular environments of deposition, such as river deltas, shallow marine sand banks or sheet-like sand bodies from storms or transgression (a rising of the sea level relative to the land).

Carbonate reservoir rock is usually found at the place of formation (in situ). Carbonate rocks are susceptible to alteration by the process of *diagenesis* which are a chemical and physical processes affecting a sediment after deposition.

---

[2] R.L.Sengbush: petroleum exploration, a quantitative introduction, library of congress 1st edition 1986. p 9: 11

The pores between the rock components, for example the sand grains in a sandstone reservoir, will initially be filled by *pore water*. The migrating hydrocarbons will displace the water and thus gradually fill the reservoir. For a reservoir to be effective, the pores need to be in communication to allow secondary migration, and also need to allow flow towards the borehole once a well is drilled into the structure.

The pore space is referred to as *porosity* in oil field terms. *Permeability* measures the ability of a rock to allow fluid flow through its pore system. Porosity is an important parameter for determining the number of hydrocarbons stored in a reservoir, and the permeability indicates how easy these hydrocarbons are to produce. A reservoir which has a good porosity but low permeability is termed "tight". [1]

3.2. Over thrust belts

Until 1975, there was plenty of interest in overthrust belts as petroleum provinces, but no success. Then, after more than 500 dry holes in the Rocky Mountain overthrust of Utah and Wyoming, in what had been called a "driller's graveyard," the Pineview field was discovered in

[1] Patrick A. Narbel • Jan Petter Hansen Jan R. Lien: Energy Technologies and Economics. Springer International Publishing Switzerland 2014. P 74

1976 in the Utah portion of the overthrust, and this was followed by the discovery of the Ryckman Creek field in Wyoming, 15 miles northeast of Evanston. The major discovery to date in the Utah-Wyoming thrust belt is the Anschutz Ranch East field in the northwest corner of Utah along the Absaroka thrust fault, thrust faults are formed by beds pushing upward along the fault face, in contrast to normal faults where the beds drop down along the face. [1]

Folding and thrusting dominate the structural style of the eastern part of the seismic profiles. The seismic profiles support the surface geology, which shows at least two major phases of deformation, a Late Cretaceous phase developed in the east resulting from the emplacement of the Oman mountains thrust sheets, and a Tertiary deformation phase resulting from the culmination of the Musandam thrust sheet. Moreover, the seismic sections suggest that the Tertiary compressional event induced the thrusting of Late Permian-Mesozoic shelf carbonates and the folding of the Late Cretaceous and Tertiary sedimentary cover.

The seismic Profile 2 shows evidence of small-offset normal faults that cut through the shelf carbonates and die out in the unconformable foreland basin sequence (Fiqa Formation). These faults are probably related to

[1] R.L.Sengbush: petroleum exploration, a quantitative introduction, library of congress 1st edition 1986. p 47

the flexural bending of the shelf carbonate sequence in response to the crustal loading during the initial phases of emplacement of the allochthons.

Seismic Profile 1 shows that foreland basin sequences (Aruma and Pabdeh Groups) are cut by relatively high angle west verging thrusts that are associated with a series of tight folds. Most of these thrusts extend deeper and offset the carbonate platform. These faults appear to merge and detach within the lower part of Late Permian—Mesozoic shelf carbonate sequence as indicated by the series of imbricate thrusts. In contrast, Profile 2 suggests the presence of a WSW-dipping high-angle east verging thrust fault underlying the tight fold of Jabal Hafit that cut through the foreland basin sequence and overlying sequences. The thrust appears to detach within the lower part of the Aruma sequence or along the top of the shelf carbonates.

The most prominent thrust is illustrated in Profile 1 and cuts through the entire Late Permian-Mesozoic shelf carbonates and show listric shape flattening into a basal detachment. The thrust causes large-scale uplift on the hanging wall of the thrust (≥ 2.0 s TWT) and juxtaposition of shelf carbonates onto Aruma Group. Major subsidence is also observed on the south-western side of the major thrust where the shelf carbonates are at ≈ 3.5 s

TWT. Significant subsidence is also seen on the north-eastern side of the uplift. In addition, the profile suggests the presence of low-displacement back thrusts that offset the top of Thamama- Wasia sequence but do not continue upward into the overlying Aruma sequence. The precise timing of thrusting and folding is debatable. However, the seismic sections show that most of thrust faults extend tip lines up into the Pabdeh and Fars Groups showing that timing of slip extended up to the post- Oligocene–Miocene and continue till present day. Moreover, in the northern UAE and west of the Musandam peninsula these thrusts are sealed by the flatlying Miocene Mishan Formation marls and clays. Therefore, our interpretation is consistent with many other studies, which correlated the thrusting and folding that resulted in the foreland basins of the UAE with the collision of Arabia with Central Iran along the Zagros Suture which started in the Late Oligocene with indentation of the Musandam peninsula and initiation of the Hagab thrust. [1]

---

[1] Khalid Al Hosani • Francois Roure • Richard Ellison • Stephen Lokier: Lithosphere Dynamics and Sedimentary Basins: The Arabian Plate and Analogues. Springer-Verlag Berlin Heidelberg 2013. P 136

Fig. 6.3 Seismic reflection profile in the immediate vicinity of well W4 showing well-to-seismic tie. Location of the well is shown in Fig. 6.1. Total depth (TD) of the well is 4,724 m, Late Triassic Gulailah Formation. Information used for well-to-seismic tie includes biostratigraphic ages, lithologies, gamma ray log. Also shown is the porosity versus depth curve resampled porosity derived from neutron porosity log

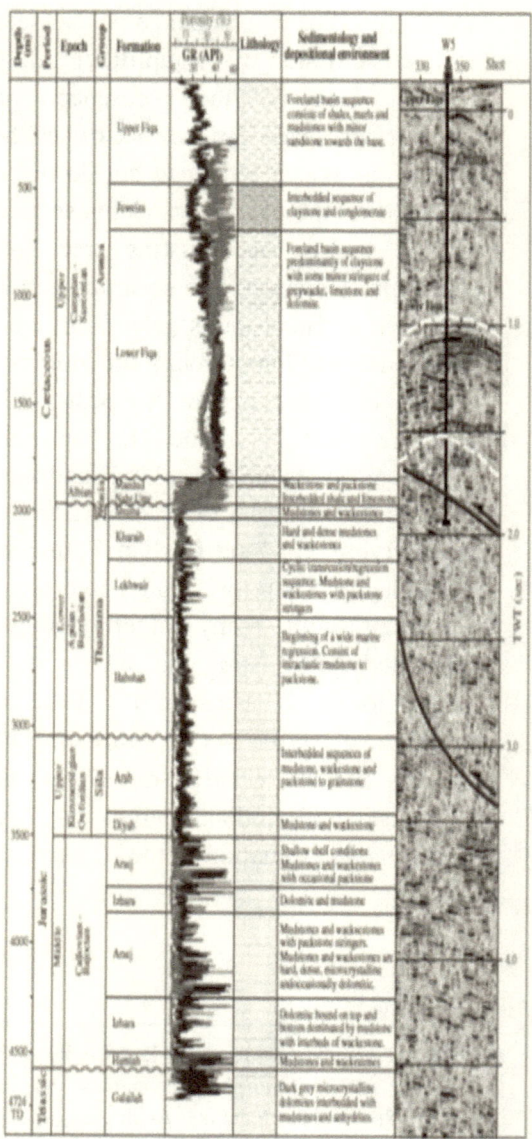

3.3. Petroleum Fractions

Oil is refined and separated into a large number of commodity products, from gasoline and kerosene to asphalt and chemical reagents used to make plastics and pharmaceuticals. 84% by volume of the hydrocarbons present in petroleum is converted into energy-rich fuels, including gasoline, diesel, jet fuel, heating, and other fuel oil and liquefied petroleum gases. The remaining oil is converted to pharmaceuticals, solvents, fertilizers, pesticides, and plastics. Therefore, petroleum is vital to many industries, and thus is a critical concern to many nations. Some common fractions from petroleum refining are: [1]

• Liquefied petroleum gas (LPG) is a flammable mixture of propane (C_3H_8) (about 38% by volume and more in winter) and butane (C_4H_{10}) (about 60% by volume and more in summer) used as a fuel in heating appliances and vehicles. Energy content of liquefied petroleum gas per kilogram is higher than for gasoline because of higher hydrogen to carbon ratio. Liquefied petroleum gas emits 81% of the CO_2 per kWh produced by oil and 70% of that of coal. Liquefied petroleum gas has a typical specific heat of 46.1 MJ/kg compared with 43.5 MJ/ kg

[1] Yasar Demirel: Energy Production, Conversion, Storage, Conservation, and Coupling. Springer-Verlag London Limited 2012. P 33: 34

for gasoline. However, its energy density of 26 MJ/l is lower than either that of gasoline. Pure n-butane is liquefied at around 220 kPa (2.2 bar), while pure propane (C_3H_8) at 2200 kPa (22 bar). At liquid state, the vapor pressure of liquefied petroleum gas is about 550 kPa (5.5 bar).

• Gasoline is primarily used as a fuel in internal combustion engines. A typical gasoline consists of hydrocarbons with between 4 and 12 carbon atoms per molecule. It consists mostly of aliphatic hydrocarbons obtained by the fractional distillation of petroleum, enhanced with iso-octane or the aromatic hydrocarbons toluene and benzene to increase its octane rating. The specific density of gasoline ranges from 0.71 to 0.77 (6.175 lb/US gal) higher densities having a greater volume of aromatics. Gasoline contains about 132 MJ/US gal (higher heating value), while its blends differ by up to 4% more or less than the average. The emission of CO_2 from gasoline is around 73.38 g/MJ.

• Petroleum diesel contains 8–21 carbon atoms per molecule with a boiling point in the range of 180–360 C (360–680 F). The density of petroleum diesel is about 6.943 lb/gal. About 86.1% of the fuel mass is carbon and it offers a net heating value of around 43.1 MJ/kg. However, due to the higher density, diesel offers a higher volumetric energy density at 128,700 Btu/gal versus 115,500 Btu/gal for gasoline, some 11% higher. The CO_2 emissions from diesel are 73.25 g/MJ, (similar to gasoline). Because of quality regulations, additional refining is required to remove sulfur which may contribute to a higher cost.

• Kerosene is a thin, clear liquid formed containing between 6 and 16 carbon atoms per molecule, with density of 0.78–0.81 g/cm^3. The flash point of kerosene is between 37 and 65 C (100 and 150 F) and its autoignition temperature is 220 C (428 F). The heat of combustion of kerosene is similar to that of diesel: its lower heating value is around 18,500 Btu/lb, (43.1 MJ/kg), and its higher heating value is 46.2 MJ/kg (19,861 Btu/lb).

• Jet fuel is a type of aviation fuel designed for use in aircraft powered by gas turbine engines. The commonly used fuels are Jet A and Jet A-1 which are produced to a standardised international specification. Jet B is used for its enhanced cold-weather performance. Jet fuel is a mixture of a large number of different hydrocarbons with density of 0.775-0.840 kg/l at 15 C (59 F). The range is restricted by the requirements for the product, for example, the freezing point or smoke point. Kerosene-type jet fuel (including Jet A and Jet A-1) has a carbon number between about 8 and 16; wide-cut or naphtha-type jet fuel (including Jet B), between about 5 and 15.

- Fuel oil is made of long hydrocarbon chains, particularly alkanes, cycloalkanes, and aromatics and heavier than gasoline and naphtha. Fuel oil is classified into six classes, numbered 1 through 6, according to its boiling point, composition, and purpose. The boiling point, ranging from 175 to 600 C, and carbon chain length, 9–70 atoms. Viscosity also increases with number, and the heaviest oil has to be heated to get it to flow. Price usually decreases as the fuel number increases. Number 1 is similar to kerosene, number 2 is the diesel fuel that trucks and some cars run on, leading to the name "road diesel". Number 4 fuel oil is usually a blend of heavy distillate and residual fuel oils. Number 5 and 6 fuel oils are called residual fuel oils or heavy fuel oils.

Carbon fuels contain sulfur and impurities. Combustion of such fuels eventually leads to producing sulfur monoxides (SO) and sulfur dioxide (SO_2) in the exhaust which promotes acid rain. One final element in exhaust pollution is ozone (O_3). This is not emitted directly but made in the air by the action of sunlight on other pollutants to form ground level ozone, which is harmful on the respiratory systems if the levels are too high. However, the ozone layer in the high atmosphere is useful in blocking the harmful rays from the sun. Ozone is broken down by nitrogen oxides. For the nitrogen oxides, carbon monoxide, sulfur dioxide, and ozone, there are accepted levels that are set by legislation to which no harmful effects are observed. [1]

From the chemical element point of view, there are only five kinds of basic elements naturally existing in petroleum compounds. They are C, H, O, N, and S elements. These elements combined with other microelement constitute the various hydrocarbon and nonhydrocarbon compounds of petroleum. The carbon and hydrogen contents in some crude oils from different places in the World. It can be noticed that the variation in the contents of carbon and hydrogen stays in a narrow range despite these crude oils came from different places and have different properties. Among these oils, the carbon content only ranges between 83 and 87 % (mass percentage), and the hydrogen content also ranges from 11 to 14 % (mass percentage). Take both elements into consideration, the total contents vary in the range of 95–99 % in general. [2]

petroleum consists of two essential kinds of compounds: hydrocarbon and nonhydrocarbon. Hydrocarbon compounds chiefly include paraffin hydrocarbons,

[1] Yasar Demirel: Energy Production, Conversion, Storage, Conservation, and Coupling. Springer-Verlag London Limited 2012. P 35

[2] Xuetao Hu • Shuyong Hu Fayang Jin • Su Huang: Physics of petroleum Reservoirs, Petroleum Industry Press, Beijing, China 2017. P 167

naphthenic hydrocarbons, and aromatic hydrocarbons (arene). Among hydrocarbons, paraffin hydrocarbons are the predominant in petroleum components. The nonhydrocarbon includes gum and asphaltene which are composed of O, N, S compounds. In general, the heavy components of crude oil are mainly constituted by nonhydrocarbon compounds.

Natural gas is basically composed of the gasiform light hydrocarbons of C1–C4; whereas crude oil mainly consists of the liquid hydrocarbons of C5–C16. The paraffin hydrocarbons, with carbon atoms higher than C17, are usually solid or semisolid. They are the major components of paraffine and asphaltene. [1]

A crude oil composed mostly of saturated hydrocarbons is termed as "paraffin base" crude. Crudes containing dominant proportions of naphthenic hydrocarbons leave a residuum of complex asphalts on distillation, and hence are termed as "asphalt-base" or "naphthenic-base" crude. Crudes between the above-mentioned are called mixed-base crudes. Generally, paraffin-base crude oils are easy to burn because they have more paraffin hydrocarbons compared with other crudes; and are the most valuable since a large percentage of

[1] Xuetao Hu • Shuyong Hu Fayang Jin • Su Huang: Physics of petroleum Reservoirs, Petroleum Industry Press, Beijing, China 2017. P 168

high-grade lubricating oils can be yielded from them.

Therefore, crude oil is generally referred to as being either "paraffin base", when it contains large proportions of paraffins, or "naphthenic" or "asphalt base" when the naphthenes are the dominant group.

Natural gas exists in nature under pressure in reservoir rocks in the Earth's crust, either dissolved in heavier hydrocarbons and water or by itself. It is produced from the reservoir similarly to or in conjunction with crude oil. [1]

Natural gas consists principally of gaseous hydrocarbons. The predominant component of a natural gas is methane (CH_4), which typically ranges from 60 to 90 %, followed by decreasing amount of ethane (C_2H_6), propane (C_3H_8), butane (C_4H_{10}), and heavier hydrocarbons which may be present as gases or vapors. The gaseous impurities are chiefly nitrogen, carbon dioxide, and hydrogen sulfide (H_2S), and traces of hydrogen, oxygen, and carbon monoxide (CO) may be present. [2]

---

[1] Xuetao Hu • Shuyong Hu Fayang Jin • Su Huang: Physics of petroleum Reservoirs, Petroleum Industry Press, Beijing, China 2017. P 169: 171

[2] Xuetao Hu • Shuyong Hu Fayang Jin • Su Huang: Physics of petroleum Reservoirs, Petroleum Industry Press, Beijing, China 2017. P 171

3.4. Well Type

Wells are drilled for exploration, appraisal or production. Exploration wells are used to find and confirm the presence of hydrocarbons, appraisal wells delineate and define the boundaries of the reservoir, and development wells are used for production. Development drilling differs from exploration and appraisal drilling in that data acquisition is no longer the primary function of the well, and instead the objective is to drill targets as efficiently as possible. MODUs are used for all well types but are the only economic option for exploration and appraisal drilling. Development wells may be drilled from MODUs or a platform rig. The time to drill in both cases are about the same, but the cost of a MODU well is significantly higher than a platform well. In deep water, the top portions of wells are often drilled ("top holes") from a MODU, and after infrastructure is installed, the remaining portion is drilled and completed from a platform rig to minimize construction cost. [1]

---

[1] Mark J.Kaiser, Brian F.Snyder: The Offshore Drilling Industry and Rig Construction in the Gulf of Mexico, Springer-Verlag London 2013. P 1: 2

4. Concept of Crude oil

Oil is less carbon-intensive fuel than coal: its carbon content is in average 85 wt.%.

As fuel, oil was introduced to the world at the turn of the twentieth century (though it was known to ancient people in many parts of the world, where crude oil naturally seeped out of the ground). Although the initial discoveries of oil at a commercial scale occurred as early as in the 1850s in Baku (Azerbaijan), Bend (Romania), Oil Springs (Canada), and Titusville (Pennsylvania, USA), oil started entering the world energy market after major oil field discoveries in early 1900s in Texas, Oklahoma, California (USA), and in the 1920s–1940s in the Middle East (Bahrain, Iraq, Iran, Saudi Arabia). The 1960s–1970s witnessed the discovery of major oil fields in Alaska (USA) and North Sea areas (UK, Norway).

Unlike coal, oil is liquid, which makes it more versatile, convenient, easily transportable, and valuable primary fuel in a great variety of applications. It also has the highest gravimetric and volumetric energy content among all fossil fuels: 46 MJ/kg and 37 MJ/L, respectively (on average). Only two of these features make oil an ultimate carbon fuel, surpassing in value all other types of fossil fuels. Oil is the greatest gift given by Nature to humankind. Just to imagine what would have happened if oil never existed on our planet and all that was available to our predecessors were only coal and gas, in all likelihood, people would have spent enormous resources to convert them into more convenient, versatile, and energy-rich liquid hydrocarbon fuels (as some countries were compelled to do that in a response to necessity).

The introduction of oil and oil-derived products to the world market led to another radical technological innovation: an internal combustion engine (ICE), which revolutionized individual, commercial, and public transport through the use of cars, buses, trucks, and first-generation aircrafts. Since mid-twentieth century, oil assumed a dominant role at the energy market as the automotive, petrochemical, and other oil-reliant industries have matured. As more and more oil was discovered and gasoline and diesel fuel driven transportation was rapidly expanding all over the world, oil's share in the world's total final energy consumption steadily grew and reached 33 % in 2011. Because of its unique properties and value, oil has become the world's strategic commodity: it is produced in a few oil-rich regions, but is shipped all over the world via pipelines, railroads, and marine tankers. No wonder, oil is sometimes called *"blood of industry."*

Crude oil is rarely used as is; so, the first step in its utilization by consumers is its preprocessing and refining at large refineries, which transform crude oil into a variety of products including motor fuels (gasoline, diesel fuel), aviation fuels (jet fuel, kerosene), and heating oil, coke, and feedstocks for petrochemical and chemical industries. Transportation sector has been and remains the major consumer of oil-derived products (consuming more than half of all petroleum products). In the USA, gasoline is the primary transportation fuel (318.5 million gallons per day), followed by diesel fuel (153.1 million gallons per day) and jet fuel (61.8 million gallons per day) (1 US gallon is equal to 3.8 l).

According to IEA, oil demand is projected to grow and reach 105.2 million barrels per day (MBD) in 2030 (1 barrel is equal to ~159 l). The transport sector will remain the main driver of the oil demand increase worldwide accounting for 97 % of the increase in the world oil use until 2030. Most of the projected increase will be covered by OPEC: its share of the world oil production will increase from the current 44 to 52 % in 2030 (OPEC stands for Organization of Petroleum Exporting Countries). Non-OPEC conventional oil production has already peaked (or is expected to peak in the near future); however, this decline will be offset by the increase in unconventional oil production.

The report from the HIS Cambridge Energy Research Associates states that oil demand in developed countries has probably already peaked and will not exceed the prerecession (2008) levels, mostly, due to the combination of several factors, such as:

• Demographics and socioeconomical changes (vehicle ownership rates in developed countries have already reached a "saturation" level).

• Introduction of more fuel-efficient vehicles (by 2016, mileage of cars and light trucks is projected to increase by 42 and 30 %, respectively).

• Introduction of new more energy efficient technologies.

At the same time, the global demand for oil from 2010 to 2020 is projected to increase by almost 14 %, mostly due to developing countries, predominantly, China and India. The report notes that China's fleet will grow from 12 million vehicles in 2005 to 110 million by 2030. The share of developing countries in the global oil demand will increase from 39 % in 1990 to 51 % by 2020, whereas the share of developed countries will drop from 61 % in 1990 to 49 % in 2020.

The current trends show that the new oil reserves that are being exploited are not only more expensive to develop and recover, but the time span between times when the well is drilled and when oil is produced becomes much longer. Currently, it takes longer for oil supply to respond to changes in oil price, which implies that the oil supply is becoming less *elastic* (*Elasticity* is the term used by economists to describe how much supply or demand would respond to changes in price.).

Worldwide, the oil supply is becoming less elastic as new oil supplies come increasingly from hard-to-reach reserves and unconventional oil. For example, Brazil's giant pre-salt fields and deep-water discoveries on the Gulf of Mexico and elsewhere are much more difficult, expensive, and slow to develop compared to past discoveries. Likewise, Canada's tar sands are expensive and slow to develop.

The USA produced 221 million barrels of crude in April 2013, with more than half coming from Texas and the Gulf of Mexico. In March 2013, Texas oil production reached its highest level since 1984. That month, the State pumped more than 74 million barrels of crude from the ground. (If Texas were a country, it would be one of the 15 largest oil producers in the world.)

Unconventional oil plays increasingly important role in the overall supply of liquid fuels to the energy market. Unconventional oil resources include extra-heavy oil, oil sands (tar sands, bituminous sands), shale oil, gas-to-liquids (GTL), and coal-to-liquids (CTL). Canadian (Alberta) oil sands and Venezuela's Orinoco Belt bituminous sands are typical representatives of unconventional oil resources. Oil sands represent a thick mixture of heavy organic matter (bitumen), sand, clay, and water. The estimates of Canadian oil sands reserves vary between 178 billion barrels and one trillion barrels. In the USA, tar sand resources are mostly concentrated in the state of Utah, and their recoverable reserves are somewhat less than that of Canadian tar sands: 12–20 billion barrels of oil.

Advantageously, tar sands in Alberta can be recovered by open pit mining technique, which substantially reduces their cost. Nevertheless, the oil recovery from tar sands is an extremely laborious and energy-intensive process: 2 tons of the sand yields only one barrel of oil, and it requires large amounts of steam and water (2–4.5 volumes of water per one volume of oil although most of the water is recycled).

Roughly, 75 % of oil (bitumen) can be recovered from the sand. Although the development of tar sands is net energy positive: providing 7–10 units of energy for every unit consumed, this index is substantially lesser than that of conventional oil.

After recovery, tar sands require chemical manipulation with heat, pressure, and chemicals to become crude oil that could be further processed to diesel, jet fuels, and other petroleum products. In order to transport the tar sands through a pipeline (e.g., from Canada to the USA), it has to be diluted with light liquid hydrocarbons to become "dilbit" (which stands for "diluted bitumen").

Oil sands have the potential to contribute to global energy security via diversification of oil supply (e.g., it makes the USA less dependent on OPEC's oil).

Increasingly higher crude oil prices would stimulate the increase in the output of the Canadian oil sands and other unconventional oil sources (For the Canadian oil sands, the profitability relies on oil prices with the threshold around $75–80 per barrel.). The global unconventional oil production is projected to increase from 1.8 MBD in 2008 to 7.4 MBD in 2030.

Recently, there have been concerns that oil sands could exact a heavy toll on the environment, and their increased production could move our planet to a disastrous tipping point for climate change. The adverse environmental impact of the oil sands industry is linked to the immense amount of water and fuel resulting in 20 % more CO_2 emissions than conventional oil on a "well-to-wheel" basis. Many experts consider oil sands as one of the dirtiest, most carbon-intensive fuels in par with coal. According to reports, CO_2 pollution from oil sands has risen 36 % since 2007. In an attempt to limit CO2 emissions from oil sands, IEA suggested that their production should not exceed 3.3 MBD, and yet approved oil sand production is projected to surpass 5 MBD (NASA's climatologist James Hansen called this move *"game over for climate change"*). Estimates indicate that just from burning Alberta's tar sands alone there will be additional temperature rise of nearly 0.4 °C.

As it stands now, tar sands are part of fossil fuel addiction. In 2011, the industry produced 1.8 million barrels per day of oil resulting in the emission of 47.1 million metric tons of CO_2 (equivalent) into the atmosphere, about 2 % more than the year before, and the production is still growing. There are, however, positive developments in the industry aiming at reducing its carbon footprint. For example, at its facilities, Shell has introduced alternative less carbon-intensive approaches to thermal cracking of bitumen that involve adding hydrogen to the process.

Additionally, Shell has recently begun deploying carbon capture and storage (CCS) technology to some of its bitumen upgraders. When completed (in 2015), the project (called

"Quest") will capture and store underground about one million metric tons of CO_2 per year. In another recent development, tar sand producers could now face carbon tax; in particular, Alberta province imposes carbon price of $15 per metric ton for any emission above a target of reducing by 12 % the total amount of GHG emitted per total number of barrels produced. Although tangible, this carbon price would unlikely compel tar sand developers to pursue CCS, because to implement the technology it would be necessary to impose a carbon price of about $100 per metric ton or even more. Therefore, any future carbon regulations may adversely affect the competitiveness of the unconventional oil industry.

According to the US Energy Information Administration (EIA), oil and NG production in the USA has jumped 14 % and 10 %, respectively, since 2008.

An oil boom the USA is experiencing now is largely due at least three main reasons:

• Breakthroughs in hydraulic fracturing and horizontal drilling techniques facilitated new oil production in rich oil shale formations in North Dakota (Bakken Shale) and Texas (Eagle Ford)

• High oil prices spurred the record investments by oil companies for new production

• Higher oil prices rendered the production of marginal oil economically viable (made possible by the first two factors)

The US oil production is projected to further increase in the near future. EIA estimates that the country's oil production will grow another 20 % by 2020, and as a result of that and higher fuel efficiency standards, the USA will reduce its share of petroleum imports from 49 % in 2010 to 38 % by 2020 to 36 % in 2035. A new oil shale formation has been discovered in California: Monterey Shale is estimated to hold 400 billion barrels of oil, according to the US Geological Survey, which is more oil than in North Dakota's Bakken Shale and nearly half the conventional oil in Saudi Arabia. But getting it out will be a challenge considering California's specific geological structure (due to the San Andres fault), which may render the horizontal drilling combined with hydraulic fracturing unpractical here. California-based company Occidental will try to utilize a new technology known as "deep acid injection" to recover shale oil. The technique involves injecting hydrofluoric or other acids deep underground, where they dissolve shale rock and allow the oil to flow. The developers claim that this method is cheaper and less controversial than fracking, since much lesser volumes and pressures are involved.

In the USA, growing oil production coupled with shrinking consumption (due to energy efficiency gains in transportation and industry) has created positive trends that may have not only economic but also geopolitical repercussions.

According to the IEA's WEO-2012 report, North America's oil supply will grow by nearly 4 million barrels per day between 2012 and 2018, amounting to nearly 50 % of the global output growth over that period. By 2020, the USA is projected to be the world's largest oil and gas producer, overtaking Saudi Arabia, and by 2030, the USA will become a net exporter of oil (most of the growth will come from drilling in the Gulf of Mexico and hydraulic fracturing of shale formations). By that time, the USA will also become self-sufficient in terms of net energy use (today, the US energy imports provide 20 % of the US energy needs).

A rapidly rising demand for oil from developing economies is another important factor in the oil equation: for the first time, developing countries are set to consume more oil that developed countries (IEA estimates that developing countries will hit 54 % of the global total by 2018, up from 49 % in 2012.). China will lead this move: its demand for oil will rise by 25 % between 2012 and 2018. Developing economies and emerging markets are also heavily investing in oil refining and infrastructure, and they will be responsible for virtually all net crude distillation capacity growth.

The IEA projects that under the right conditions the world could produce increasing amounts of oil through 2035 and potentially meet the world's growing demand for oil. The key here is "under the right conditions," because the main challenge here is that the world will unlikely produce familiar (conventional) crude oil at the rate it did at the peak of crude production (ca. 2005). In the IEA's 2012 Outlook scenario, increasing world's population accompanied with the rising standards of living in the developing countries would push the oil demand from 87.4 MBD in 2011 to 99.7 MBD in 2035. The scenario projects that to meet this demand oil-producing countries would have to double their production of unconventional oil. In particular, the USA would have to triple its production of tight oil (trapped in nearly impermeable rocks, which would require tens of thousands of new hydro fractured wells) and bring it to 3.2 MBD in 2020. This will become economically feasible only with continued high oil prices.

Besides tight oil, NG liquids (NGL) will be another major player in the IEA's future liquid fuel supply scenario. Although NGL are mostly a by-product of NG production, typically, they are lumped with crude oil and generalized as "liquids" (NGL include the range of hydrocarbons from the lightest ones that could be liquefied only when pressurized, e.g., C_3H_8, C_4H_{10}, to larger molecules that could exist as liquid at atmospheric pressure and are present in crude oil, e.g., C_5–C_7 hydrocarbons). Currently, almost half of all NGL are converted into petrochemicals and plastics, with the remainder almost equally split between transportation and fuel usage applications. IEA projects 50 % increase in NGL production by 2035 with significant part of it going to the transportation sector. The experts are concerned that money will be the most uncertain factor in the IEA scenario. IEA predicts the price of oil rising to $125 per barrel in real terms by 2035, which will help fund the maintenance of crude oil production and drive up unconventional oil production and facilitate transportation's shift to NGL-based fuel. For this to happen, OPEC would have to restrain its production, while non-OPEC production would surge to allow prices to rise. It is too early to say if this scenario will be even plausible given geopolitical circumstances on the ground. [1]

The origins of oil are not completely understood, but there is a consensus that the following conditions must be satisfied if an oil

[1] Nazim Muradov: Liberating Energy from Carbon: Introduction to Decarbonization. Springer Science+Business Media New York 2014. P 7: 11

deposit is to be formed. There must have been a supply of organic material from either plants or animals. Oxygen must have been excluded from the environment. There must have been a supply of sediment sufficient to contain the organic matter to prevent its dispersal.

There must have been bacteria present that could use the organic matter as food thus transforming it chemically. Petroleum deposits have a great deal of oxygen removed from their compounds, presumably taken by these bacteria to sustain themselves.

The low concentrations of oxygen in fossil fuels are responsible for their efficiency as an energy source. It is still not clear what exactly the mechanism has been for the formation of large underground deposits of oil. A better understanding of the source would help geologists determine where to dig to find it.

The first well in the United States was dug in Pennsylvania in 1859. By 1864 there was a sufficient worldwide market for oil so that 20 million tons were shipped from the United States. The largest exploration conducted in the 19th century was in the Baku fields in Azerbaijan of the former Soviet Union. The oil from these still producing fields led to the founding of the giant petroleum companies, Shell Oil, Royal Dutch, and British Petroleum. Before the motor car age, the principal use of oil was for illumination, especially in lamps. The lightest fraction, what is now its most important component, gasoline, was discarded. [1]

Oil is a naturally occurring flammable liquid consisting of a complex mixture of hydrocarbons of various molecular weights, which define its physical and chemical properties, like heating value, color, and viscosity. The composition of hydrocarbons ranges from as much as 97% by weight in the lighter oils to as little as 50% in the heavier oils. The proportion of chemical elements varies over fairly narrow limits. The hydrocarbons in crude oil are mostly alkanes, cycloalkanes and various aromatic hydrocarbons while the other organic compounds contain nitrogen, oxygen, sulfur, and trace amounts of metals. The relative percentage of each varies and determines the properties of oil. [2]

• Alkanes, also known as paraffin, are saturated hydrocarbons with straight or branched chains containing only carbon and hydrogen and have the general formula C_nH_{2n+2}. They generally have from 5 to 40 carbon atoms per molecule. For example, CH_4 represents the methane, which

[1] Sidney Borowitz: FAREWELL FOSSIL FUELS Reviewing America's. Energy Policy. Plenum Press, New York in 1999. P 54: 55

[2] Yasar Demirel: Energy Production, Conversion, Storage, Conservation, and Coupling. Springer-Verlag London Limited 2012. P 32

is a major component of natural gas. The propane (C_3H_8) and butane (C_4H_{10}) are known as petroleum gases. At the heavier end of the range, paraffin wax is an alkane with approximately 25 carbon atoms, while asphalt has 35 and up. These long chain alkanes are usually cracked by modern refineries into lighter and more valuable products.

• Cycloalkanes, also known as naphthenes, are saturated hydrocarbons which have one or more carbon rings to which hydrogen atoms are attached according to the formula C_nH_{2n}. Cycloalkanes have similar properties to alkanes but have higher boiling points.

• Aromatic hydrocarbons are unsaturated hydrocarbons which have one or more six-carbon rings called benzene rings with double and single bonds and hydrogen atoms attached according to the formula C_nH_n.

Oil currently supplies more than 40% of our total energy demands and more than 99% of the fuel are used in transportation. Known oil reserves are typically estimated at around 1.2 trillion barrels without oil sands, or 3.74 trillion barrels with oil sands. [1]

---

[1] Yasar Demirel: Energy Production, Conversion, Storage, Conservation, and Coupling. Springer-Verlag London Limited 2012. P 33

Petroleum (from Greek "rock oil") is sometimes used to mean just oil, but technically petroleum means oil and gas and some semi-solid components.

"Conventional" petroleum means oil and gas derived from geologic deposits, usually found and exploited using drill bit technology with the resources moving to the surface because of their own pressure or with additional pressure supplied by pumping additional natural gas or water into the reservoir. "Unconventional" petroleum includes shale oil, tar sands, some bitumen, and coal-bed methane. These resources are often "undercooked" (oil sands) or "overcooked" (tar sands) by geological forces, and/or of a less concentrated nature (for example mixed with sand) or found in deposits in very deep or hostile environments. A somewhat gray area is "previously uneconomic" oil and gas which is usually a lower grade resource of any kind that was traditionally not worth exploiting, but becomes commercially exploitable when oil prices are high, with "new" technologies such as horizontal drilling, and with the depletion of easier to exploit and cheaper traditional reservoirs.

Essentially all unconventional oil requires more energy to extract. Humans have tended to exploit the large, high quality and easy oil deposits first. This is an example of the "best first" principle introduced by the Nineteenth century economist David Ricardo. Today about half of the oil we extract comes from only three percent of the oil fields, most of which have been exploited for 50 or more years. Onshore deposits in places such as Texas and Louisiana were developed long before deeper offshore regions. But the large onshore resources are now depleted, and there are more than 4000 very expensive platforms in the Gulf of Mexico off Louisiana and the mouth of the Mississippi River that are responsible for much of the United States' remaining oil and gas production.

Exploitation of the North Sea deposits has involved similar, expensive technology. Over time we are moving further and further off shore, and deeper and deeper in the sediment, and are finding on average smaller fields. As of this writing arctic exploration and development has been postponed because of the large expense and disappointing results so far, combined with the fall in the price of oil since mid-2014. [1]

- **Classification of Crude Oil at the Surface**

Commercial value of petroleum liquid can be estimated quickly through the measurement of the following physical characteristics: relative density (specific gravity), gasoline and kerosene content, sulfur

[1] Charles A.S. Hall: Energy Return on Investment. 2017. P 41: 42

content, asphalt content, pour point, cloud point, and so on. Therefore, crude oils at the surface are often classified by its physical properties. The common classifications are listed as follows: [1]

Classification by the Relative Density of Dead Oil:

Light oil: relative density <0.855, °API > 34;
Conventional oil: relative density: 0.855–0.934, °API: 34-20;
Heavy oil: relative density >0.934, °API < 20.

Classification by the Content of Resin-Asphaltene:

In crude oil, resin-asphaltene can form colloidal structure, which has great influence on the flowability and other physical properties of crude oil, and thus leads to high-viscosity crude oil.

Less-resin crude: the content of resin-asphaltene in crude oil less than 8 %;

Resin crude: the content of resin-asphaltene in crude oil ranges from 8 to 25 %;

High-resin crude: the content of resin-asphaltene in crude oil higher than 25 %.

---

[1] Xuetao Hu • Shuyong Hu Fayang Jin • Su Huang: Physics of petroleum Reservoirs, Petroleum Industry Press, Beijing, China 2017. P 175: 178

In general, the crude oils produced from most oil fields in China are "less-resin crude" or "resin crude".

Classification by Wax Content:

The paraffin content in crude oil often affects its freezing point. Generally, the higher the paraffin content is, the higher the freezing point. High freezing point will cause a lot of troubles during the production and the gathering–transportation of crude oil.

Less-wax oil: the wax content in oil less than 1 %;

Waxy crude oil: the wax content in oil ranges from 1 to 2 %;

High-wax oil: the wax content in oil higher than 2 %.

The wax content of crude oil from oil fields in China changes in wide range. Most crude oils are "high-wax oil" while some crude oils are "less-wax oil".

Classification by Sulfur Content:

The sulfur contained in crude oil is harmful. It erodes steel products and is not favorable for oil refining. In addition, the sulfur dioxide generated after oil burning will pollute atmosphere. So, some countries clearly prescribe that crude oil products cannot be sold until the sulfur contained in oil has been removed.

Less-sulfur crude: the sulfur content in oil less than 0.5 %;

Sour crude oil: the sulfur content in oil is between 0.5 and 2 %;

High-sulfur crude: the sulfur content in oil higher than 2.0 %.

Classification Based on Oil Composition:

This classification is mainly based on the composition of crude oils, namely on the amount of paraffins, naphthenes, and aromatic compounds along with nonhydrocarbon compounds (i.e., resins and aspbaltcncs) in oils.

Paraffin-base crude oil: They contain normal and isoalkanes and less than 1 % S. The asphaltene and resin contents are below 10 %. Percentage of aromatic hydrocarbons is low. They yield gasoline of low octane number and oil of high cetane value. They give high-grade lubricating oils on distillation and leave behind paraffin wax as residue. The oil tends to have high API and pour point and is green in color. Paraffin-base crude oils represent 2 % of the world's oil supply.

Naphthene-base crude oil: They contain cycloalkanes (naphthenes). Asphaltic matter is present in quite large proportion. Paraffinic wax is very little or absent.

These crude oils yield good quality gasolines and asphalts/bitumens. Asphalt-base crude oil is dominated by the naphthenic hydrocarbon compounds. The oil is black in color and tends to have low °API and a low pour point. Asphalt-base crude oil represents about 15 % of the world's oil supply.

Paraffin – naphthene-base crude oils/mixed-base crude oil: They have both paraffinic and naphthenic hydrocarbons together with a certain proportion of aromatic hydrocarbons. On distillation, they yield residue containing both paraffin (waxes) and asphaltic matter, their density and viscosity are more than paraffinic class.

Classification by Viscosity:

Viscosity is one of the most important properties of in-place oil. Oil viscosity controls the off-take potential of oil wells, and affects the ultimate recovery of oil reservoirs.

Low-viscosity crude: the viscosity of oil in reservoirs lower than 5 mPa s; Medium-viscosity crude: the viscosity of oil in reservoirs between 5 and 20 mPa s; High-viscosity crude: the viscosity of oil in reservoirs between 20 and 50 mPa s; Viscous crude oil: the viscosity of oil in reservoirs higher than 50 mPa s; its relative density is higher than 0.920.

Special Classification:

Condensate oil: it means the oil produced from the gas reservoirs, in which liquid oil will condense when reservoir pressure is lower than a special pressure named dew point pressure. This kind of gas reservoir is known as condensate gas reservoirs. The relative density of condensate oils is about 0.75, lower than that of black oils.

Volatile oil: it contains a relatively large fraction of lighter and intermediate components which vaporize easily. They behave liquid-like at reservoir conditions. The reservoir temperature of a volatile oil is near the critical temperature. In production, the liquid oil is easily volatile and shrinking when it is brought to the surface. Generally, its gas–oil ratio is in the range of 210–1200 m^3/m^3. The relative density of the oil is less than 0.825, and its volume factor is higher than 1.72.

High pour point oil: the crude oil whose pour point is higher than 40 °C. Pour point means the lowest temperature, expressed as a multiple of 5 °F, at which the liquid is observed to flow when cooled under prescribed conditions. Cloud point is the temperature at which paraffin wax begins to solidify and is identified by the onset of turbidity as the temperature is lowered. Both tests qualitatively measure the paraffin content of the liquid.

5. Concept of Natural Gas

Gas hydrates, or clathrate hydrates, exist in a solid, ice-like form that consists of a host lattice of water molecules enclosing cavities occupied by molecules of guest gases. Common guest gases in gas hydrates include CH4, C2H6, C_3H_8, i-C_4H_{10}, CO_2, and H_2S; they also include other gases such as Ne, Ar, Kr, Xe, N_2, O_2, and hydrocarbons such as cyclopropane. Gas hydrates can be categorized into Structure I, II, and H according to the type of cavity in the host lattice. Each cubic meter of gas hydrates can hold approximately 160 m³ of natural gas at standard temperature and pressure. Gas hydrates stay stable under certain thermodynamic conditions, i.e., low temperatures and high pressures. Such a condition can be provided by geologic formations such as permafrost and suboceanic sediments. Most marine gas hydrates are formed of microbially generated gas. In general, gas hydrates can contain different guest molecules in different cages, depending on their sizes and the availability of guest molecules under given thermodynamics conditions. But methane is the prevalent gas in natural gas hydrates. Therefore, many studies under the name of gas hydrates are actually directed to methane hydrate.

Gas hydrates are important energy sources mainly due to the huge number of hydrocarbons in concentrated forms they contain. Of primary interest are the hydrates that contain combustible low molecular weight hydrocarbons such as methane, ethane, and propane. According to Makogon, there are tremendous amounts of natural gas trapped in hydrates in the permafrost and the continental shell in the ocean around the globe. Worldwide, gas hydrate was estimated to hold about 1016 kg of organic carbon in the form of methane. The surveys by the US Geological Survey (USGS) have estimated that reserves of methane in hydrate form exceed all the other fossil fuel forms of organic carbon. Therefore, naturally occurring gas hydrates on the earth, containing mostly methane, have the potential to become a major source of energy in the second half of the 21st century. Gas hydrates have aroused great interest in disciplines such as chemical engineering, chemistry, earth sciences, and environmental sciences. But in fact, gas hydrates were initially regarded as a source of problems in the energy industry because the conditions under which oil and gas are produced, transported, and processed are frequently conducive to gas hydrates formation. Recently, considerable concern over the potential threat of gas hydrates to the global environment has been raised because of the great greenhouse effect of methane. It was argued that release of the large volumes of greenhouse gas stored in hydrates into the ocean and atmosphere may have played a role in the past climate change. Besides, rapid hydrate dissociation may lead to landslides along continental margins as well as other geohazards. (1)

In a narrow sense, natural gas is a combustible gas that is buried in deep ground and mainly composed of hydrocarbon compounds. 166

Natural gas is a mixture of hydrocarbon gases that occurs with petroleum deposits, principally methane together with varying quantities of ethane, propane, butane, and other gases, and is used as a fuel and in the manufacture of organic compounds. Natural gas is a gaseous mixture consisting mainly of methane trapped below ground; used extensively as a fuel. (2)

Broadly speaking, natural gas refers to all gases naturally generated in nature. In fact, not all-natural gases from reservoirs are hydrocarbon gases. Some are exactly the nonhydrocarbon gases of high purity, such as N_2, CO_2, etc. For example, the content of H_2S in a natural gas, which is from the fourth member of Shahejie and Kongdian formations in

(1)Congrui Jin • Gianluca Cusatis: New Frontiers in Oil and Gas Exploration. Springer International Publishing Switzerland 2016. P 51

(2)Xuetao Hu • Shuyong Hu Fayang Jin • Su Huang: Physics of petroleum Reservoirs, Petroleum Industry Press, Beijing, China 2017. P 167

Paleogene in Zhao Lanzhuang structure of Jizhong Depression in North China, is up to 92 %. In Sha touping gas field of Sanshui Basin in Guangdong, China, and the content of CO_2 is up to 99.75 %. [1]

Natural gas is a naturally occurring mixture of low-molecular-weight hydrocarbons and nonhydrocarbon gases found in porous formation underground. It is nearly everywhere considered to be the gaseous phase of petroleum. However, the properties of natural gas are considerably different from liquid petroleum because there is greater distance between the molecules in natural gas than in crude oil. For example, pressure has much greater effect on the density of a natural gas than on oil's density. The notable features of natural gases are much easily compressible and flowable. [2]

Natural gas is a naturally occurring mixture, consisting mainly of methane. Natural gas provides 23% of all energy consumed in the world. The International Energy Agency predicts that the demand for natural gas will grow by more than 67% through 2030. Natural gas is becoming increasingly popular as an alternative

[1] Xuetao Hu • Shuyong Hu Fayang Jin • Su Huang: Physics of petroleum Reservoirs, Petroleum Industry Press, Beijing, China 2017. P 167

[2] Xuetao Hu • Shuyong Hu Fayang Jin • Su Huang: Physics of petroleum Reservoirs, Petroleum Industry Press, Beijing, China 2017. P 210

transportation fuel. Typical theoretical flame temperature of natural gas is 1960 C (3562 F), ignition point is 593 C.

Natural gas is a major source of electricity production through the use of gas turbines and steam turbines. It burns more cleanly and produces about 30% less carbon dioxide than burning petroleum and about 45% less than burning coal for an equivalent amount of heat produced. Combined cycle power generation using natural gas is thus the cleanest source of power available using fossil fuels, and this technology is widely used wherever gas can be obtained at a reasonable cost. The gross heat of combustion of one cubic meter of natural gas is around 39 MJ and the typical caloric value is roughly 1,000 Btu per cubic foot, depending on gas composition.

Liquefied natural gas exists at -161 C (-258 F). Impurities and heavy hydrocarbons from the gaseous fossil fuel are removed before the cooling process. The density of liquefied natural gas is in the range 410–500 kg/m^3. The volume of the liquid is approximately 1/600 of the gaseous volume at atmospheric conditions. [1]

"Petroleum" includes natural gas liquids and natural gas. Natural gas is often

---

[1] Yasar Demirel: Energy Production, Conversion, Storage, Conservation, and Coupling. Springer-Verlag London Limited 2012. P 35

found associated with oil, although it has other possible sources, including coal beds and organic-rich shales. We get natural gas when the original plant material, with molecules often of hundreds to thousands of carbon atoms linked together, has been "cracked" or broken by geological energies to a length of five or fewer carbon atoms, becoming most usually methane, with one carbon atom surrounded by four hydrogen molecules. Once distribution systems are built, gas is an ideal fuel as it is easy to handle and very useful. Since oxidizing hydrogen releases more energy per unit carbon dioxide produced, its use would contribute less to climate change than other fossil fuels, at least if not much of it leaks from the wells and pipes (methane has a global warming potential of 28–84 times higher than carbon dioxide per molecule. When natural gas is held in a tank some heavier fractions fall out as natural gas liquids, and these materials can be used either directly or as inputs to refineries. While natural gas was once considered an undesirable and dangerous byproduct of oil production and flared into the atmosphere, with time a complex pipeline system evolved and now natural gas more or less ties with coal as the second most important fuel in the United States and the world. An important question is: if oil supplies falter can natural gas take over its role? While it is not as energy dense or transportable as oil it comes close, and because it is relatively clean and malleable it has many special uses such as a fuel for baking and as a feedstock for plastics and nitrogen fertilizer. Natural gas is used increasingly to make "clean" electricity, although it is possible that our grandchildren will be unhappy about this if they need that gas for higher value uses such as making fertilizer. [1]

NGH is a crystalline material composed of water molecules that form cage structures and gas molecules that occupy almost all of the cages, the whole being stabilized by the weak electrical force, van der Waals bonding. NGH is directly analogous to metallic and other economic mineral deposits formed by crystallization from mineralizing solutions. This differentiates it strongly from gaseous and liquid (including tar sands) hydrocarbon deposits.

Naturally occurring NGHs are composed predominantly of methane, and NGH is often referred to as 'methane hydrate even in the absence of analyses, but appreciable heavier hydrocarbon gases such as ethane, propane, and butane may occur where thermogenic gases have contributed to the gas flux.

Because the crystalline cage structures closely pack the gas molecules, one m3 of

[1] Charles A.S. Hall: Energy Return on Investment. 2017. P 42

Structure I methane NGH will produce about 160 m^3 of methane (at STP), equivalent to an energy density of over 165,000 BTU/ft^3. This compression factor, regardless of seafloor depth and ambient pressure, is a principal component of the economic value system for NGH. Compound NGH, formed from mixed or higher density natural gases, will have less gas per m3 than methane-NGH but increased BTU content determined by the gas mixture. Compound NGH formed from a mixture of gases is more stable (at lower pressures and higher temperatures) than pure methane-NGH.

NGH forms spontaneously when the right combinations of elevated pressure and low temperature conditions exist, and when a suitable concentration of hydrate-forming gas can mix with and react with water. NGH is commonly found within a gas hydrate stability zone (GHSZ) that extends from near a cold surface on land or the seafloor downward to some depth at which increasing temperature renders NGH unstable. Although NGH is generally stable in the ocean water at great depth, it will not survive there because it will float upward due to its low density (about 0.9) and will dissociate when it passes through the phase boundary. The temperature of the water column in the open ocean decreases with depth as a result of the cold, dense, saline water produced as a byproduct of freezing ice.

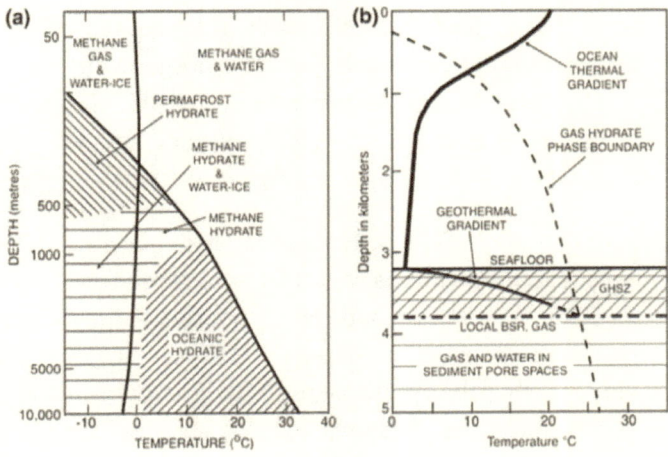

In the Arctic Ocean, the water temperature at depth is at or below 0 °C, which places the minimum water depth for NGH stability at about 250 m water depth. We prefer to assume a depth of about 300–350 m for the minimum depth of a continuous or year-round GHSZ in the Arctic Ocean Basin sediments. As the water depth increases, and pressure increases, the GHSZ increases in thickness.

In general, thicker GHSZ sections are more likely to have more significant NGH concentrations. In addition, geothermal gradients, which describe the average change in temperature with depth over specific intervals, may vary considerably.

Oceanic NGH differs from all other types of natural gas deposits in being responsive to changes in its environment. The greater part of the hydrocarbon gases in NGH appears to have been generated at depth from organic matter either biogenically or thermosgenically and has been transported upward into the GHSZ, driven by tectonic forces or dewatering of the sediment pile driven by compaction.

High TOC sediments can also generate considerable local gas, but TOC-rich sediments tend to be muddy and have poorly defined permeability paths. In these, NGH-forming gas moves primarily by diffusion in the groundmass or by flow in fractures. Deep sources are particularly obvious when the gas has a thermogenic signature containing a mixture of higher-density hydrocarbon gases.

NGH may occur at any level within the GHSZ, depending on the nature of the 'plumbing system' utilized by groundwater and natural gas to bring the mineralizing solutions into the GHSZ from the sediment pile. High-grade, but more broadly distributed and deeper NGH concentrations, in which the mineralization is directly related to gas transported by water movement into permeable strata in the GHSZ suggests that mineralizing solutions migrated along porous geological horizons that passed up into the GHSZ. Higher level and isolated concentrations suggest that faults or fracture systems, along which water flow may be much faster, are able to bring the mineralizing solutions higher in the GHSZ before crystallizing in a favorable host strata or vein work. For instance, fractured shale carrying substantial NGH in vein works occurs in close proximity to sand-hosted NGH concentrations in the northern GoM.

When the gas reaches the GHSZ, in which pressure and temperature are suitable for NGH formation, NGH will form so long as the gas concentration in the pore water media is high enough. As the dissolved gas concentration rises and falls, the hydrate growth dynamic alters and greater or lesser amounts of hydrate may form. Free gas is usually associated with groundwater that is saturated or supersaturated with dissolved gas. If the dissolved gas concentration falls below a certain level, usually identified as the vapor pressure of the hydrate forming gas in the hydrate, the hydrate will dissolve. Thus, NGH is not a material that is fixed to a particular geological attribute over time. It occurs only within a GHSZ, and as that may change thickness or position depending on sedimentary deposition or erosion, the presence of NGH within it also will migrate from an area in which NGH is unstable and into an area where it is stable, as may happen when sea level rises and pressure increases, or sediment erosion takes place. NGH may reposition itself by a process of recrystallization.

NGH is very environmentally responsive, being able to crystallize, dissociate and dissolve, migrate, and recrystallize when environmental conditions change.

Under conditions of continued sedimentation, for instance, the base of the GHSZ will move upwards because it is keyed to the sediment surface. The balance between the seafloor low temperature and the rising temperature with depth is maintained. NGH that was once within the GHSZ at its base will convert naturally to gas when it passes out of the field of NGH stability and either pond or tend to rise into the GHSZ where it can form more NGH. A fall in sea level will also lower pressure on the seafloor, causing the base of GHSZ to rise. In contrast, sediment erosion will cause the temperature gradient to move deeper into the sediment and lower the base of the GHSZ, as will rise in sea level that raises the pressure. When NGH migrates with the GHSZ in order to maintain its thermodynamic stability, it may leave behind virtually no definitive evidence of its one-time presence.

Seafloor warming will cause thinning of the GHSZ while seafloor cooling will cause thickening: these are the environmental changes usually associated with methane release or greater sequestration. Changes in pore water salinity or chemical composition, while probably relatively rare, have the potential to move the position of the NGH phase boundary. Concentration, of course, is key; if the concentration of the dissolved NGH-forming gas falls sufficiently, dissolution takes place.

Four general classes of NGH in different surroundings have been identified (Table 3.1). These classes are based on thermodynamic models that were used to estimate the costs of processes that are required to convert NGH to its constituent gas and water. There are subtle but important differences in the petroleum systems related to each of these classes of NGH concentration.

Note that the presence of a geological trap is not one of the criteria for any NGH class.

NGH concentrations that may prove economic may only be found in a GHSZ thick enough to host significant concentrations with enough overlying sediment to stabilize the reservoir by its weight during drilling, NGH conversion, and gas extraction. Depending on the sediments within the GHSZ and the presence and disposition of NGH, there is a wide range of geotechnical possibilities. For instance, the presence of multiple NGH-enriched units that can be mechanically very strong when NGH concentrations are high, essentially binding the sediment grains into a solid aggregate or where sediment grains may be cemented together

Table 3.1 NGH classification

Class	NGH	Bounded	Materials in contact	Geological situation	System
1	Concentrated	Permeability boundaries/ geological strata	Gas (over water)	1a Oceanic	Open
				1b Oceanic, Permafrost	Closed
2			Mobile water	Oceanic	Open
3			No gas or water	Dry gas trap (including vein-type NGH)	Closed
4	Dispersed	Few permeability boundaries	Pore water	Fine-grained marine sediments	Very open

Revised from Moridis and Kowalsky (2006)

by thin NGH films, can affect overall sediment stability. The minimum thickness of a GHSZ necessary to host a prospective producing NGH deposit is not known.

An NGH prospect and its host and overlying sediments will have to undergo geotechnical analysis as part of developing a production plan. With time and experience, less conservative safety margins will probably emerge. Although it is not known to what water depths possible NGH concentrations may occur, there will probably be some maximum depth below which exploration cutoffs will apply for either operational considerations or some aspect of NGH paragenesis.

Ideally, large concentrations of NGH are most likely to be found near the base of relatively thick GHSZs in which the sediment will be more compacted under the influence of gravity than in shallower sediments with thinner GHSZ. The more compacted nature of the NGH host sediments and particularly the degree of compaction and reduced permeability of sediments bounding a sand-hosted NGH deposit may strongly control the percentage of technically and economically recoverable natural gas. NGH will generally occur worldwide in semi-compacted sediments that do not have the geologically strong character of conventional natural gas reservoirs. The stronger the geomechanical character of the reservoir sediments and between the NGH deposit and the seafloor, the lower the risk of mechanical failure and more likely higher rates of NGH conversion and natural gas production. [1]

- **Classifications for Natural Gas**

Natural gas is often found associated with oil in all oil-producing fields of the world, whereas it is also found in many gas fields in the complete absence of oil. So, it may be broadly classified as associated when it occurs with oil, and as nonassociated when it occurs alone. Distinctly, associated gas coexists with oil in an oil reservoir. But it may be present in the form of solution gas in the oil, or in the form of gas-cap gas, laying above the oil in the reservoir. [2]

Sometimes, natural gas produced from a gas reservoir may contain small number of

[1]Michael D. Max · Arthur H. Johnson William P. Dillon: Natural Gas Hydrate – Arctic Ocean Deepwater Resource Potential. 2013. P 19: 23

[2]Xuetao Hu • Shuyong Hu Fayang Jin • Su Huang: Physics of petroleum Reservoirs, Petroleum Industry Press, Beijing, China 2017. P 178

heavier hydrocarbons that are separated as a liquid called condensate oil. A natural gas containing condensate is said to be wet or rich gas depending on the number of heavier hydrocarbons in the gas. Conversely, a gas is called dry or poor gas if no liquid hydrocarbon condenses from the gas when it is extracted to the surface. If the number of acidic components (e.g., carbon dioxide, hydrogen sulfide) in gas is higher than 1 %, the gas is called sour; otherwise called sweet. [1]

---

[1] Xuetao Hu • Shuyong Hu Fayang Jin • Su Huang: Physics of petroleum Reservoirs, Petroleum Industry Press, Beijing, China 2017. P 178

6. Conventional and Unconventional Resources

Oil and other fossil fuel resources cannot be replenished on a timescale of interest to humans. Oil was formed during periods of extreme global warming millions of years ago. At that time, algae and zooplankton multiplied in warm, sunlit waters, converting solar energy via photosynthesis into organic material composing their bodies. Upon their death, their organic remains slowly settled in the stagnant (anoxic) ocean depths forming thick layers of organic matter. Later, sediments washed in by rivers buried this organic material preventing it from being oxidized by air, thereby preserving it. Over time, this material was buried deeper and deeper and slowly "cooked" by increased temperature and pressure, changing it first into a waxy material called kerogen and then with more heat into liquid and gaseous hydrocarbons. During the process, called catagenesis by petroleum geologists, long-chain hydrocarbons are broken into shorter ones.

The temperatures and pressures needed for oil formation occur at depths between 2286 (7500 feet) and 4572 m (15,000 feet) called the "oil window". If too cool, oil remains trapped in the rock as keragen (shale oil); and, if too hot, oil is converted to natural gas (primarily methane) by thermal cracking. So, why is oil often found closer to the surface? Surface erosion can bring it closer, or oil, once liberated from the source rock, can migrate upward and even appear on the surface as seeps. Oil can also be trapped in porous reservoir rock beneath an impermeable cap rock, such as shale. These porous rocks form oil reservoirs and consist of sandstone or ancient coral reefs that hold oil like a sponge. Most oil "traps" are anticlines that form when the overlying cap rocks are buckled by tectonic movement forming a dome that traps the oil. If the reservoir is large enough, it forms an oil field from which oil can be extracted by drilling and pumping through the overlying rock layers. [1]

Oil and gas is generated from organic-rich rocks by thermogenic or biogenic processes. When such "source rocks" are exposed over periods of geologic time to high temperatures the organic material breaks down releasing oil and gas that then migrate toward the surface due to buoyancy. The temperature required for thermal maturation of a source rock varies depending on the type of organic material but the minimum temperature for oil generation is approximately 50 C and for gas generation is 100 C. Most thermogenic oil and gas are generated at depths of 2–6 km.

(*)J. Edward Gates • David L. Trauger • Brian Czech: Peak Oil, Economic Growth, and Wildlife Conservation. Springer Science+Business Media New York 2014. P 7: 8

Methane may also be produced from source rocks by the biogenic breakdown of organic material in source rocks. Such biogenic gas is produced at lower temperatures and at shallower depths. Whether of thermogenic or biogenic origin, oil and gas can be trapped by buoyancy in "reservoirs" in porous rocks beneath an impermeable layer of rock typically at depths of over 1 km. The permeable nature of the host rock, high pressures related to depth of burial, and the concentration of oil and gas in discrete reservoirs allow relatively easy extraction of oil and gas by drilling wells. Until the 1990s almost all the world's oil and gas production was produced from such "conventional" fields. Natural gas in conventional fields may occur with ("associated gas") or without ("nonassociated gas") oil.

In either case the gas may contain compounds that can be separated at the surface as liquids. Natural gas liquids (NGLs) such as propane, butane, and pentane are sometimes included in reporting oil production but are not insignificant: they comprise, for example, 3.5% of the total energy production of the United States.

Estimates of the world's original endowment of conventional oil and gas resources have tended to increase because of the advances in technology over time. Advances in geologic concepts, drilling technologies, seismic imaging, and computer modeling using large datasets have progressively revolutionized the search for oil and gas over the last century. Likewise, advances in production technologies, pipeline construction, and tankers have all made resources available that at one time would have been considered economically unviable. Advances in science and technology allow more oil and gas to be found in old fields, within existing petroleum provinces, and in new frontier regions.

Existing oil and gas fields that have already been in production for years may, at first blush, seem unusual sites to look for further reserves. However, the US Geological Survey (USGS) in 2000 estimated that 48% of the oil and 41% of the natural gas that remains to be added to reserves in the future lie within existing fields. Increases in successive estimates of the estimated recoverable oil and gas are known as "reserve growth." On average, only 22% of the oil is currently recovered from fields worldwide. There are many reasons for such a low percentage. Much of the oil within a reservoir rock will not easily move toward wells. Enhanced recovery methods such as gas reinjection, water-flooding, and flushing with polymers and surfactants can free up more of the oil. While such secondary and tertiary recovery methods are commonly used in mature oil fields in developed countries, they are not yet widely used in many other regions. Another reason for reserve growth is that there is rarely a single reservoir within an oil or gas field as most are split into numerous compartments, each containing amounts of oil/ gas in varying amounts. Advances in seismic imaging over the last 20 years have allowed not only good visualization of these compartments but also the fluids within the compartments. At the same time, technological advances allow drilling with much greater precision permitting access to much smaller subsurface targets over time. While it will never be possible to economically drain all the oil and gas out of a field, recovery rates of over 70% may eventually be feasible in many areas Much oil and natural gas also remains to be found in undiscovered fields within existing petroleum provinces. The largest fields tend to be discovered early in the exploration history of a basin and progressively smaller ones are found over time.

The infrastructure that is built to develop the larger fields allows fields to be developed that would otherwise be too small to justify the construction of pipelines, platforms, ports, and processing facilities. By analogy estimates can be made of the number and size of remaining undiscovered fields from the discovery history of a petroleum province. This methodology may underestimate the total resource if more than one type of oil and gas accumulation is present. For example, the discovery of giant oil and gas fields in the subsalt regions in offshore regions of the Gulf of Mexico added a new "play" in what was thought to be a mature oil province.

There is a strong possibility that further major accumulations of conventional oil and gas will also be found in frontier basins where little or no exploration has taken place. Most of the potential areas are in regions of Deepwater or harsh climates.

Over time technological advances have made exploration feasible in areas once thought inaccessible. This has been particularly true in the ability to drill to deeper depths. In 1960 any drilling in water depths over 20 m was regarded as "Deepwater" but by 1980 oil fields had been found in over 300 m water depth, by 1990 in over 850 m water depth, and by 2010 in over 2,400 m water depth. Total drilling depths also increased dramatically with a record set in 2009 with the discovery of the giant Tiber oil field in the Gulf of Mexico which is at 1,200 m water depth, with a total drilling depth of 10,680 m. In the last decade giant oil fields have been found in ultra-Deepwater areas not only in the Gulf of Mexico but also offshore West Africa and Brazil. The giant Brazilian Tupi field lies not only in Deepwater (>2,000 m) but also below a 2,000 m thick layer of salt. It is only recently that seismic technology has allowed an understanding of the structures below thick salts and drilling technologies have permitted drilling through such strata.

As in the past, technological advances will permit exploration for oil and gas in frontier regions currently regarded as inaccessible. Future exploration in Deepwater will likely lead to more significant discoveries. Outside the Atlantic realm other regions with potential for Deepwater exploration include offshore East Africa, the Great Australian Bight, and offshore New Zealand. There is a growing interest in the potential of the Arctic region where geologists believe there are substantial oil and gas resources but where the severe climate, ice floes, and icebergs all make exploration and development hazardous and, in many areas, either prohibitively expensive or impossible using currently available technologies. [1]

Another major factor in estimating future availabilities of exhaustible resources is the difference between 'conventional' and 'unconventional' occurrences (e.g. extra heavy oils, oil shale, tar sands, coal-bed methane, shale gas, methane clathrates or uranium dissolved in sea water). These terms lack standard definitions but are often used, which adds greatly to

(¹)Anupama Malhotra: Fossil Energy Springer Science+Business Media New York 2013. P 12: 14

(¹)Ferenc L. Toth: Energy for Development Springer Science+Business Media Dordrecht 2012. P 154 misunderstandings, especially in the debates on peak oil, gas or coal. [1]

As the name suggests, unconventional resources generally cannot be extracted with technology and processes used for, say, conventional oil, which is usually understood as crude oil capable of flowing under normal conditions, i.e. oil with an API value greater than 20°. (API is an arbitrary scale designating an oil's specific gravity, a proxy for viscosity. The API scale equates high specific gravity values to low API gravity values, and vice versa.) Unconventional resources require different logistics and cost pro fi les, and pose different environmental challenges. Their future accessibility is, therefore, a question of technology development, i.e. the rate at which unconventional resources can be converted into conventional reserves (notwithstanding the demand for liquid fuels and relative costs). As new production methods are developed that allow unlocking unconventional resources at increasing rates, thus making them conventional mainstream products, the distinction between unconventional and conventional becomes meaningless. In short, like the boundary between conventional reserves and resources, the boundary between conventional and unconventional resources is in permanent flux. [2]

---

[2]Ferenc L. Toth: Energy for Development Springer

There is a great deal of excitement and debate as of the second decade of this century about whether "unconventional" (but light, good quality) oil from, for example, the Bakken formation in North Dakota and the Eagle Ford field in Texas, and natural gas from shales such as the Marcellus shale can continue to provide an energy renaissance for the United States. Production of oil in the U.S., which had been falling since 1970, increased rapidly from 2008 to 2014 and almost reached a new record. Since mid-2015 though, with oil prices falling and the best areas heavily exploited, oil production has been falling again. While the amount of oil in these formations is enormous, the rocks (actually sandstone, not shale) have low porosity (pore space) and permeability (ability of oil to flow through the formation) so that only some 5 % of the oil in place can be extracted even by new, energy intensive "heroic" efforts. This compares with an average of some 38 % from conventional fields. The new technologies include horizontal drilling (with up to 2mile lateral extensions) and the shattering or "fracking" of the rocks with very high-pressure water and chemicals. This has allowed considerable amounts of previously inaccessible oil and gas to be produced. Optimists predict one hundred years of gas and that the US will soon export oil (as of 2016 it imports half of its use). But so far most of this "unconventional" oil and

Science+Business Media Dordrecht 2012. P 155

gas has come from a relatively few "sweet spots," so the total production may go through nearly a full exploitation cycle in just a few decades. When large claims are made, as for Monterrey oil, it is always good to have a competent geologist such as Hughes take a look. Meanwhile most estimates for total global oil and gas production suggest peaks and then declines within a decade or two, with or without unconventional sources. [1]

Meanwhile conventional gas production in the United States has peaked and declined to less than half the peak, so that so far, the unconventional gas of all kinds is mostly compensating for this decline. Where it falls short, imported gas bridges the gap. Thus, while fracked oil and natural gas is likely to be very important as conventional oil production and availability declines, it is likely to extend the petroleum age by only a few decades. both unconventional and total oil production in the United States have already gone through a secondary peak and are declining "Heavy" (i.e., long chain, high molecular weight) oil tends to be relatively "overcooked" compared to conventional "light" oil, is very abundant in Canada and Venezuela, and can be exploited by digging out the heavy oil or the "tar sands" and treating it with natural gas to add hydrogen and

---

[1] Charles A.S. Hall: Energy Return on Investment. 2017. P 42: 43

make the oil more fluid. This is, in general, an inefficient and capital—and energy—intensive process. Nevertheless, the technology to exploit these deposits exists, the resources are large (but again of varying quality) and are likely to continue to supply a modest quantity of petroleum to the world. The exploitation of Canadian tar sands is especially well developed, but their extraction has been declining since 2014 with the decline in the world price of oil. [1]

But conventional oil is not the only type of oil in the market place. Unconventional oil and natural gas liquids (NGLs) already supplement conventional oil supply in meeting rising global demand for liquid fuels (what markets demand and not oil per se). Unconventional oil resources are much more abundant than conventional oil reserves and resources. Their production is technically, economically and environmentally more challenging than conventional oil, but with growing demand expectations and sufficiently high market prices unconventional oil will be increasingly called upon to supplement conventional oil. In the past, human engineering ingenuity, technology change and innovation have countered upstream cost pressures and this is expected to continue. After all, 'knowledge is truly the mother of all resources'. Including

---

[1] Charles A.S. Hall: Energy Return on Investment. 2017. P 43: 45

unconventional oil resources and NGLs changes the potential global oil production profile.

Uncertainty as to the availability of unconventional oil is the timely investment in their production capacities as the oil produced would face the highest marginal costs, possibly an order of magnitude or more than the cheap conventional oil of the Middle East. In the recent past, investment in oil production capacity has not been a high national policy priority in several oil-exporting countries. Geopolitical market manipulation in a fragile market situation (e.g. opening pumps in the short run) could flood the market with cheaper oil and put the investment in unconventional oil at risk. [1]

In understanding the rise in oil price since 2004, and also the limits to future oil supply, an important distinction to make is between the production of conventional oil and that of non-conventional oil.

Oil exists in many forms. It can be found at the land surface or on the seabed as oil seeps; in degraded form in tar pits and in extensive areas of tar sands; as oil's precursor, kerogen, still in the original rock in which it was laid down (and from which it needs retorting to yield 'oil shale'

---
[1] Ferenc L. Toth: Energy for Development Springer Science+Business Media Dordrecht 2012. P 155: 156

either still captured in the original rock (as 'shale oil', that needs hydraulic fracturing, 'fracking', to release it); or after having migrated to an open-pored reservoir of rock (an oil field), from which it can be extracted by drilling.

It is this last class of oil, the relatively light, flowable oil in fields that is generally classified as conventional oil, and where the bulk of oil production currently, and by far the largest part historically, has been of this class of oil.

By contrast, non-conventional oil tends to be found in extensive regions (within which there may be 'sweet spots'), and where flow to a production well is not possible without significantly changing the nature of the oil itself (for example, by heating to reduce viscosity, addition of a solvent, or retorting), or that of the surrounding material (such as mining the sand in which the oil is contained, or by fracturing the rock in which it is trapped). Non-conventional oil thus includes very heavy oil, oil from tar sands and Venezuela's Orinoco fields, shale ('light tight') oil and oil produced from kerogen by retorting.

Oil, in addition, can be produced from yet other sources. It can come from the physical transformation of some of the gas from gas fields, as either condensate or natural gas liquids ('NGLs'); by chemical transformation of gas from a variety of fossil sources (yielding gas-to-liquids, GTLs), or similarly from coal (coal-to-liquids, CTLs); or alternatively from biomass, either directly as biofuels, or by chemical or biological change from a variety of types of biomass.

Note that NGLs are often included in conventional oil (though in this book we try to break them out separately where possible), while the oil produced from GTLs, CTLs and biomass is often classed as 'other liquids'. Annex 1 gives more detailed definitions.

To see why this distinction between classes of oil is important, we need to ask the following question: Why over a century and a half has the world, in the main, used conventional oil (i.e. oil in fields), rather than oil from the many other sources that exist, and where some of the latter (such as oil from biomass, and from coal and kerogen) were used extensively before conventional oil came to dominate?

The answer is simple: Up to now the oil in fields has usually been far cheaper to produce than these other oils. The reason for this generally lower cost of conventional oil relates principally to flow rate, and energy return.

❖ Flow rate

As noted above, oil in fields is concentrated geographically and flows easily, and hence often yields large flow rates when produced by relatively simple drive mechanisms, such as own pressure, gas drive or water flood.

For example, while the 1859 Drake well, the first commercial oil well in the US, yielded up to about 20 barrels of oil per day ('b/d'), only 2 years later the first major US gusher yielded 4000 b/d, and in 1901 the Spindletop field in Texas flowed at 100,000 b/d. Admittedly in these early years such flows were often short-lived, but subsequent large fields typically have yielded over 500,000 b/d for considerable periods; while the Middle East giants produce 1 million b/d and above, and the world's largest field, Ghawar, averages over 5 million b/d. Thus, once located, conventional oil from large oil fields has generally been cheap to produce due to relatively easy production methods and high flow rates.

As a result, while 'the petrol tank in your car does not care' what type of oil (conventional or non-conventional) is used, the user certainly does. The user would far prefer conventional oil at its pre-1973 long-term average real-terms price of $15/bbl, or even at its post-1985 real-terms average price (up to the 2004 increase) of $30/bbl, than to have to pay the*$60/bbl production cost for US light tight oil,1 or the more than $160/bbl for 'Canada oil sand mine upgraded' oil, currently estimated by IHS-CERA; or the production cost—whatever it will be—of retorted kerogen oil plus carbon capture, or of synthetic fuel made from electrolysis of water plus CO_2.

❖ Energy return

Another way to look at the relative ease of production of conventional oil is in terms of its energy return; nearly all of the non-conventional oils have lower energy returns. Though the data are hard to establish unequivocally, Guilford et al.

(2011) and Hall (personal communication) suggest for example that in the US the ratio of energy return to energy invested (EROI) for conventional oil was about 30:1 in the 1930s, rising to 40:1 in the 1970s as scale increased and technology improved, and subsequently falling with production of the more difficult conventional oils, such as deep offshore or Arctic oil, to an average ratio of perhaps 14:1 today. By contrast, nearly all non-conventional oils have lower energy ratios; tar sands, for example, being quoted as having ratios of from 1.5 to 8:1, and corn ethanol as only perhaps 2 or 3:1 (probably higher in Brazil, and in some cases perhaps negative). Since Hall et al. (2009) and Lambert et al. (2014) calculate that modern society will have difficulty in functioning if its fuels have energy ratios of less than perhaps 5–

10:1, the current transition from mainly conventional oil to increasing quantities of non-conventional oil is significant, and needs to be understood. [1]

As oil was still solidifying its leading role, in the mid-twentieth century, NG emerged as a new player and a major competitor in the energy and industry markets, and it is still gaining momentum. NG is the lightest and cleanest (from carbon emissions viewpoint) form of fossil fuels: its carbon content averages at about 76 wt.%. According to IEA, humankind is now entering the *"Golden Age of Gas"*—a tribute to an ever-increasing role of gas on the global energy arena combined with its environmental advantages over other fossil fuels.

In most cases, NG occurs near crude oil reservoirs forming a gas cap between oil and a capping (impervious) rock. At high pressure, NG is dissolved in oil and is released when oil is pumped out to the surface (more often than not, this gas is combusted at the site forming the so-called gas flares). Being gas, it can also migrate through the porous layers of the Earth's crust and accumulate in locations with favorable temperature and pressure conditions. Drilling gas wells is generally less expensive and faster than drilling for oil, and there are more gas wells

[1] R.W. Bentley: Introduction to Peak Oil. Springer International Publishing Switzerland 2016. P 3: 4

than oil wells in some countries, e.g., in the USA.

Methane (CH_4) is the main component of NG with its content typically varying in the range of 70–90 vol.%. Other light hydrocarbons (ethane, propane, butane) and (in many cases) CO_2 are also present in NG along with small amounts of N_2, He, H_2S, and water vapor. H_2S (due to its toxicity and chemical aggressiveness) and CO_2 (due to its capacity to lower NG heating value) are the most undesirable components in NG, and they are usually removed from NG before its transport or liquefaction.

Liquefied petroleum gas (LPG, mostly consisting of propane and butane) can be recovered during NG processing. NG can be conveniently and economically transported by pipelines, or it can be liquefied, stored, and transported in refrigerated vessels by railroads or designated marine tankers.

NG is widely used in a number of important industrial and residential applications, such as power generation, transportation, industrial and residential heating, and chemical feedstock for production of fertilizers, rubber, plastics. Over the last half century, the world's NG production steadily increased, and in 2011, it accounted for 23.6 % of total global energy consumption. The demand for NG is projected to continue to grow at about 1.5 % per year with new gas-fired power stations using combined-cycle technology accounting for the most of the increase. Today, nearly all projections through the middle of twenty-first century and beyond show the role of gas (especially, unconventional gas) in the global energy supply increasing and that of coal and oil decreasing.

Unconventional gas sources include shale gas, tight sand gas, coal bed methane (CBM), and methane hydrates. In contrast to conventional gas, which is extracted from porous sandstones and carbonate formations, where it has been trapped under impermeable caprocks (seal), unconventional gas is typically recovered from low-permeability reservoirs such as tight sand formations, coal seams, and fine-grained

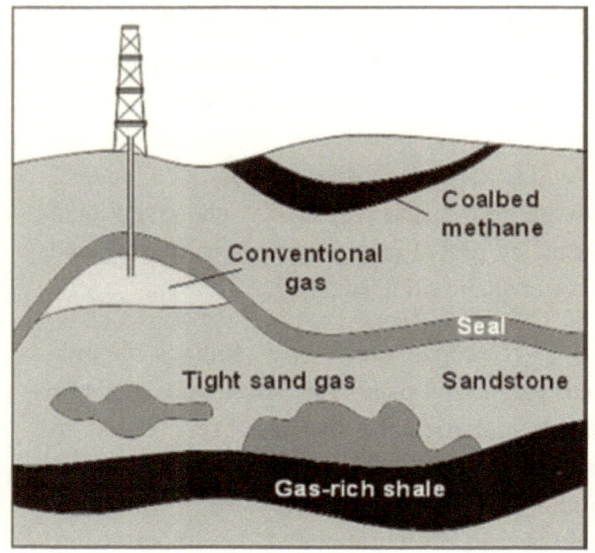

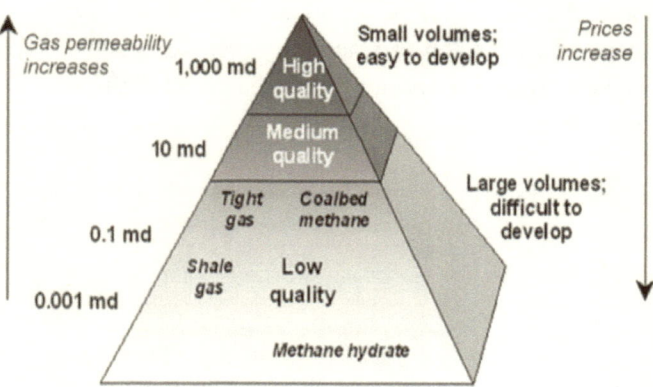

gas-rich shale rocks. The difference between conventional and various types of unconventional gas (except methane hydrates) is depicted in the Fig. Typically, shale gas occurs in rocks of Paleozoic and Mesozoic age, whereas tight sand gas could be found in sandstone formations where it gets trapped due to inability to further migrate upward. CBM is formed during the transformation of organic matter to coal over a geological time span. The Figure depicts NG resource pyramid, which elucidates the interrelation between gas resource, gas permeability, and the cost of gas recovering from sources.

It can be seen that high-quality gas (typically, of conventional type) has the lowest resource base, and it is characterized by high gas permeability and,

Table 1.1 The estimates of ultimately recoverable resources of unconventional gas and production costs

Unconventional gas source	Ultimately recoverable resources (in TCM)	Production cost (in US$/GJ)
Shale gas	204	2.9–6.7
Coal bed methane	118	2.9–7.6
Tight gas	84	2.9–7.6

subsequently, lower cost of recovery. All unconventional gas formations have much larger resource base, but they are characterized by very low permeability which drastically limits the extraction of methane gas by off-the-shelf methods and requires additional (usually, expensive nontraditional) techniques to achieve economical flow rates of gas. As a result, shale gas is much costlier to produce than conventional gas from wells due to the use of expensive hydraulic fracturing and horizontal drilling equipment.

The IEA's 2012 report provides the estimates of NG-proven reserves and recoverable resources as follows (in trillion cubic meters, TCM): 232 (with 28 in OECD and 205 in non-OECD countries) and 790 (with 193 in OECD and remaining in non-OECD countries), respectively (OECD stands for the Organization for Economic Cooperation and Development). The estimates of ultimately recoverable resources of unconventional gas and the range of production costs are presented in Table 1.1.

According to the IEA's estimates, in combination, conventional and unconventional gas resources could sustain gas production for over 250 years at the current consumption rate. Advantageously, the gas resource base is geographically well spread over the globe with every region having at least 75 years' worth of gas at current consumption rate, which has very important geopolitical implications. Countries with the largest share of unconventional gas produced by 2035 will be the USA (shale gas), China (CBM and shale), Canada (shale), Australia (CBM), India (CBM and shale), and Russia (tight gas).

The worldwide production of unconventional gas (shale, tight sand, and coal bed) is rapidly picking up the pace. In the USA, the share of shale gas of total gas supply increased from about 1 % in 2000 to 20 % in

2010 and to 30 % in 2011. According to the US EIA 2011 report, technically recoverable shale gas resources of onshore lower 48 states amount to a total of 21.2 TCM of gas with the largest shares in the Northeast (63 %), Gulf Coast (13 %), and Southwest (10 %), respectively. The largest shale gas plays are in Marcellus (11.6 TCM, or 55 % of the total), followed by Haynesville (2.1 TCM, or 10 % of the total), and Barnett (1.2 TCM, 6 % of the total). Since 2005, NG prices in the USA are lower than that of crude oil. Besides the USA, shale gas development is rapidly increasing across several regions of the world such as the UK, China, Poland, Ukraine, Australia, and Brazil. The US EIA reported that China has the world's largest shale-gas reserves estimated at 36 TCM.

According to the IEA's GAS Scenario projections, global primary NG demand will increase from 3.3 TCM in 2010 to 5.1 TCM in 2035 (about 50 % increase) and will account for 25 % of the world's energy mix (overtaking coal between 2025 and 2030). The estimates of the increase in gas production in the USA vary from 20 % (according to EIA) to 100 % (according to the US Geological Survey).

Some optimistic analysts project that shale gas will fuel the USA for the next century, but more cautious estimates predict that the US and Canadian gas production will likely peak sometime between 2020 and 2040. Nevertheless, it is evident that the gas reserves are much greater than previously thought, and taking into account cleanness of gas compared to coal and oil, many experts believe that it has enormous potential to provide economic and environmental benefits for the society.

But, on the other hand, there are concerns that the large-scale development of shale gas could cause different types of environmental problems. [1]

6.1. Tar Sands or Extra Heavy Oils

Heavy oil is highly viscous, "cold syrup" like hydrocarbons which are formed much the same way as the conventional low viscous oil. The oil sands or tar sands are loose sand or partially consolidated sandstone containing naturally occurring mixtures of sand, clay, and water, saturated with a dense and extremely viscous form of petroleum technically referred to as bitumen. In the Athabasca sands in Alberta, Canada there are very large amounts of bitumen covered by little overburden, making surface mining the most efficient method of extracting it. The overburden consists of water-laden muskeg (peat bog) over top of clay and barren sand. ~~The oil sands themselves are~~

[1] Nazim Muradov: Liberating Energy from Carbon: Introduction to Decarbonization. Springer Science+Business Media New York 2014. P 11: 15

typically 40–60 m deep, sitting on top of flat limestone rock.

Due to the high viscosity, heavy oil is more expensive to extract than conventional oil. The bitumen in tar sands cannot be pumped from the ground in its natural state.

Therefore, surface mining, requiring large areas, has been the preferred extraction technique. After excavation, hot water and caustic soda (NaOH) is added to the sand, and the resulting slurry is piped to the extraction plant where it is agitated and the oil skimmed from the top. Provided that the water chemistry is appropriate to allow bitumen to separate from sand and clay, the combination of hot water and agitation releases bitumen from the oil sand, and allows small air bubbles to attach to the bitumen droplets. The bitumen froth floats to the top of separation vessels, and is further treated to remove residual water and fine solids. About two tons of oil sands are required to produce one barrel (ca. 1/8 of a ton) of oil. Originally, roughly 75% of the bitumen was recovered from the sand but today extraction plants recover well over 90 % of the bitumen in the sand.

Several techniques which restrain from occupying large surface land areas have also been employed, e.g. Cyclic Steam Stimulation (CSS). In this method, the well is put through cycles of steam injection, soak, and oil production. First, steam is injected into a well at a temperature of 300–340 °C for a period of weeks to months. Then, the well is allowed to sit for days to weeks to allow heat to soak into the formation.

Later, the hot oil is pumped out of the well for a period of weeks or months. In the Steam assisted gravity drainage (SAGD) process, two parallel horizontal oil wells are drilled into the formation, one about 4–6 m above the other. The upper well injects steam, and the lower one collects the heated crude oil or bitumen that flows out of the formation, along with water from the condensation of injected steam. The basis of the process is that the injected steam forms a "steam chamber" that grows vertically and horizontally in the formation.

The heat from the steam reduces the viscosity of the heavy crude oil or bitumen which allows it to flow down into the lower wellbore. SAGD has proved to be a major breakthrough in production technology since it is cheaper than CSS, allows very high oil production rates, and recovers up to 60 % of the oil in place.

Several more exotic techniques have also been tried at the tar sand fields. For example, using solvent instead of steam to separate the bitumen from the sand, or an in-situ combustion process which ignites oil in the reservoir and creates a vertical wall of fire moving from the "toe" of the horizontal well toward the "heel", which burns the heavier oil components and upgrades some of the heavy bitumen into lighter oil right in the formation.

The cost of producing one barrel of tar sands or extra heavy oil amounts to between 30 and 60 Euro2008/bl of oil equivalent, to which transport costs must be added. With current oil prices (70 Euro2008/bl in September 2013), it makes economic sense to extract this resource. It has been estimated (perhaps conservatively) that, given the existing technology and current oil prices, 1–1.5 trillion barrels of tar sands and extra heavy oil can be recovered economically (IEA 2013b), most of them being located in Canada and Venezuela.

All production methods of oil from tar sand requires large amounts of energy, chemicals and water. It also releases considerable amounts of CO_2 into the atmosphere.

An upheaval of large land areas and substantial pollution is often the result. Needless to say, there are strong environmental concerns regarding extraction of energy from these resources. However, with increasing oil prices, tar sands and extra heavy oil are considered important from an industrial perspective, especially since the resource base is significant. [1]

Oil sands are rocks that consist predominantly of sandstones which contain bitumen within the pore spaces that has been produced by the biodegradation of oils in the subsurface. Most oil reservoirs are sufficiently hot that biogenic activity is curtailed or absent. However, oil that migrates into shallow reservoir rocks may be altered completely to bitumen that is very viscous. Although found close to the surface, production of oil from oil sands is expensive. The bitumen must be heated before it will flow and commercial extraction requires large amounts of energy. Once extracted the bitumen must also be upgraded by purification and hydrogenation before it can be refined like conventional crude oil.

Although oil sands have long been recognized and used in limited ways, it is only within the last 40 years that commercial production has grown. Canadian oil sands production began in 1967 and production has grown steadily. By 2009 production from oil sands was equivalent to over 550 million barrels of oil, accounting for 49% of Canada's oil production in 2009. Though production was

[1] Patrick A. Narbel • Jan Petter Hansen Jan R. Lien: Energy Technologies and Economics. Springer International Publishing Switzerland 2014. P 107: 110

initially subsidized, production costs have fallen with technological advances and is now economically viable at $50/barrel and production is forecast to more than triple by 2025. Venezuela also has substantial oil sand deposits and smaller accumulations are known in Russia and the Middle East. [1]

6.2. Non-Conventional Oil and Gas

Unconventional oil is produced or extracted using techniques other than conventional oil wells. It refers to tar sands, ultra-Deepwater oil, coal to liquids, oil shale, and natural gas liquids (NGL). Some unconventional forms of oil are extracted through processes similar to mining. I will mention three that many in the energy industry feel have great potential.

Oil Sands Oil or tar sands are composed of clay, sand, water, and oil-rich bitumen

Strip mining or open pit techniques or underground heating can be used to remove the bitumen for refining into oil. The process includes extraction and separation of the bitumen from the other materials in the tar sands. Because bitumen is heavy black viscous

[1]Ripudaman Malhotra: Fossil Energy. Springer Science+Business Media New York 2013. P 15

oil, it is mixed with lighter hydrocarbons for transport via pipelines.

One of the largest deposits is the Athabasca Oil Sands of Alberta, Canada; another is the Orinoco extra heavy oil deposit in Venezuela. This oil has been partially biodegraded by oil-eating bacteria and is still in the process of escaping, but vast amounts are still present. Canada currently has a large-scale, commercial oil sands industry. Oil sands are mined and transported to an extraction plant, where hot water and agitation are used to extract the bitumen, where it is skimmed off. Additional processing is needed to remove residual water and solids. It is then transported and eventually upgraded to synthetic crude. Two tons of oil sands can produce one barrel of oil. In situ extraction includes steam and solvent injection, and firefloods in which injected oxygen is used to burn the oil sands to produce heat needed for extraction. Large amounts of both water and energy are needed in these extraction methods. Mining and processing of oil sands have considerable impacts on wildlife and their habitats, as well as air and water quality.

Oil Shales Oil shales are source rocks that have never been buried deep enough to convert their kerogen to oil (http://ostseis.anl.gov/guide/oilshale/, accessed 13 September 2010). They are known as the "rock that burns." Oil shales have to be mined and heated to a high temperature in a process called retorting. The resultant liquid can then be separated and collected for processing. Because of the added energy needed to extract this oil, it is more expensive than conventional oil. The largest deposits of oil shale are found in the USA in the Green River Formation that covers portions of Colorado, Utah, and Wyoming. Oil shale can be mined underground the spent shale must then be disposed of in surface impoundments or as fill. Mining and processing involve a variety of environmental impacts that add to the cost. An in-situ conversion process is being developed by at least one major oil company using underground electric heaters placed in drilled vertical shafts. Heating the rock will take 2–3 years to reach temperatures of 340–370 °C (650–700 °F) at which point the oil will be released from the shale. It can then be collected in wells within the heated zone. Underground barriers called "freeze wells" would have to be created around the perimeter of the extraction zone by pumping refrigerated fluid down the well to prevent groundwater from entering and hydrocarbons from leaving the extraction zone. This complicated and expensive process is unproven at this time and would involve a variety of impacts to wildlife and air and water quality.

Tight Oil It is important to note at the beginning of this discussion that tight oil is not the shale oil of the Green River Formation; but, oil found in the Bakken Shale Formation in North Dakota and Montana and the Eagle Ford Shale in Texas. Unlike shale oil, this oil is confined by impermeable rock and has a medium to light viscosity. Advances in drilling technology have allowed some of this oil to be produced economically. Production involves both vertical and horizontal drilling in conjunction with multistage hydraulic fracturing, or "fracking." A fluid, consisting primarily of water with a small percentage (0.5–2 %) of additives, is pumped under pressure into the wellbore to open voids in the rock. The additives are designed to lubricate and prevent biofouling and corrosion. Sand or ceramic beads are then pumped into these small openings to hold them open, allowing the oil to flow to the wellbore. This process is done in multiple stages along the wellbore. Conventional methods are then used to produce the well. Since 2012, production of tight oil was the major reason for the resurgence of oil production in the USA.

For this oil play, high initial production rates are typically followed by steep declines. The productivity of new wells drops by 60 % after 1 year, leveling out to less than 40 % in the second year, less than 30 % in the third year, and so forth.

Overall field decline is about 40 % per year. As highly productive "sweet spots" are depleted, more and more wells will have to be drilled in less productive areas just to maintain production. Although the inflection point or peak can be pushed into the future by increasing the number of drilling rigs and further technological advancements, diminishing returns to scale and the depletion of sweet spots are likely to slow the rate of growth.

This scenario is similar to the Red Queen's race in Lewis Carroll's *Through the Looking-Glass,* where Alice and the Red Queen have to run very fast just to stay in place or twice as fast as that to get somewhere. How long this tight oil race can be maintained is subject to debate. Based on the maximum number of available drilling locations for the Bakken and Eagle Ford tight oil plays, Hughes predicted that production will peak by 2017, and then fall by 30–50 % per year thereafter. Environmental concerns exist over leakages of hydraulic fracturing fluids and its effect on water quality as well as changes in land use and fragmentation of wildlife habitats from increases in drilling pads and access roads. [1]

Note first that for non-conventional oils, and also the other liquids such as gas or coal to liquids, and biofuels, in the main none of the concepts of field, field size distribution (and

[1] J. Edward Gates • David L. Trauger • Brian Czech: Peak Oil, Economic Growth, and Wildlife Conservation. Springer Science+Business Media New York 2014. P 8: 9

hence discovery effort) and field decline are relevant, and hence neither is the concept of 'mid-point' peaking for production of these liquids. So, while production of a non-conventional oil or other liquid may indeed peak, it will be from different causes than for conventional oil.

For these non-conventional oils and other liquids, mostly the potential resources are very large, and for almost all, their locations are already known so exploration costs are low. (The exception on resource size is biofuels, because of competing requirements for food and biodiversity.)

However, there is a range of constraints likely to limit production of these fuels. These include

– technological readiness;

– a high investment requirement, typically, per barrel produced;

– other resource requirements (energy, water, land for waste);

– net-energy related cost and energy yield factors;

– CO_2 emissions.

Note that the availability of investment for non-conventional fuels is not straightforward. When the general energy price raises, the cost of all fuels, including the alternatives, also tends to rise because of the energy embodied in bringing these fuels on-stream. This effect was demonstrated for tar sand extraction costs during the 1970s oil shocks, for oil from shale (kerogen oil) as reported in Stobaugh and Yergin, and more recently across a range of alternative fuels. The concept was also a key factor in the original Limits to Growth modelling.

And if the energy price becomes also more volatile, then investment in alternative fuels is further discouraged, even during periods of lower price. In the following, we look at three aspects of non-conventional oil supply of current focus: the availability of light tight oil; the decline in energy return on energy invested (EROEI); and CO_2 emissions, and hence the concept of 'stranded' fossil fuel assets.

	Conventional	Shale ('tight')	Total
Oil (Gb)	3012	345	3357
Gas (Tcf)	15,583	7299	22,882
Gas (Gboe)	3000	1400	4300

The above data, in 'years of global supply at current use rates' translate to:

	Conventional	Shale ('tight')	Total
Oil ('years of supply')	95	10	~100 yrs
Gas ('years of supply')	130	60	~200 yrs

6.3. Properties of Unconventional Crude Oils

Petroleum or crude oil is a naturally occurring heterogeneous and complex mixture of organic compounds, mainly water-insoluble aliphatic and aromatic hydrocarbons of various molecular weights. Although there is not a strict definition for unconventional crude oils, the main properties that distinguish them when compared with conventional light oils are their high viscosity and density. Unconventional oils are characterized by a heavy molecular composition, containing low percentages of low molecular weight compounds. They also contain high levels of heteroatoms (sulfur, nitrogen and oxygen) and heavy metals (nickel, iron, copper and vanadium) when compared with light oils.

The American Petroleum Institute (API) gravity, a measure of how heavy or light a petroleum liquid is compared to water, is a parameter commonly used to classify oils according to their density. The API gravity is calculated as follows: [1]

$$°API = \frac{141.5}{\rho} - 131.5$$

---

[1]Kirsten Heimann • Obulisamy Parthiba Karthikeyan Subramanian Senthilkannan Muthu: Biodegradation and Bioconversion of Hydrocarbons. Springer Science+Business Media Singapore 2017. P 338: 339

where q is the density of the oil. Although the API gravity is a dimensionless parameter, it is often expressed in degrees. According to their API gravity, crude oils are classified as light (API gravity > 31.1°), medium (API gravity between 22.3° and 31.1°), heavy (API gravity between 10.0° and 22.3°) or extra-heavy (API gravity < 10.0°). This means that extra-heavy oils have a density greater than water (more than 1000 kg/m^3)

The carbon/hydrogen (C/H) mass ratio is another parameter commonly used to express the quality of crude oils. Unconventional oils are in general characterized by high C/H mass ratios (above 6.5 and sometimes even up to 11) due to a high concentration of aromatic compounds. [1]

The complex nature of unconventional oils makes the study of their molecular composition difficult and expensive. As in the case of conventional oils, SARA fractionation has been widely used to characterize them. This methodology separates crude oil into four main fractions (Saturates, Aromatics, Resins and Asphaltenes) according to their different polarity and solubility.

---

[1] Kirsten Heimann • Obulisamy Parthiba Karthikeyan Subramanian Senthilkannan Muthu: Biodegradation and Bioconversion of Hydrocarbons. Springer Science+Business Media Singapore 2017. P 339

Saturates are light components of crude oil, and consist mainly of non-polar alkanes with linear or branched chains, and aliphatic cyclic paraffins. Aromatics are species with one or more aromatic rings linked with aliphatic chains, and normally contain embedded heteroatoms. Aromatics have a similar molecular weight as saturates (450–550 g/mol), but a higher C/H mass ratio. Resins are operationally defined as the fraction of crude oils that is soluble in heptane and pentane, but insoluble in liquid propane. Despite the lack of well characterized molecular structures, resins are mainly polar, poly-nuclear molecules composed of aromatic rings, aliphatic side chains and heteroatoms. Their molecular weights vary from 700 to 950 g/mol. [1]

Asphaltenes are the heaviest and more polar fraction of crude oil; they are soluble in aromatic solvents (such as benzene and toluene) but insoluble in nalkanes. The chemical constituents of asphaltenes are similar to those of resins but with a higher molecular weight, and contain higher amounts of heteroatoms and heavy metals. The molecular structure of asphaltene molecules has been an enigma for several decades due to their complexity and their tendency to form aggregates, which presents

[1] Kirsten Heimann • Obulisamy Parthiba Karthikeyan Subramanian Senthilkannan Muthu: Biodegradation and Bioconversion of Hydrocarbons. Springer Science+Business Media Singapore 2017. P 339

difficulties in studying them. Their molecular weights, for instance, were reported to spread over a wide range, from less than 10^3 to 10^9 g/mol, which can be explained by the formation of complex aggregates. There still exists uncertainty regarding if asphaltene molecules consist of one single polycyclic aromatic hydrocarbon (PAH) or several cross-linked PAHs, known as the island and archipelago model of asphaltenes, respectively. Nowadays, the most widely accepted model refers the asphaltene molecules as containing one single, moderately large fused aromatic hydrocarbon ring linked to peripheral alkyl groups. [1]

The SARA content of unconventional oils from different reservoirs around the World varies considerably. However, in general, these oils contain low levels of saturates and high percentages of aromatics, resins and asphaltenes. The higher the content of asphaltenes and resins in the oil, the heavier and more viscous the oil is. Furthermore, the asphaltenic fraction and its strong intermolecular interactions, which form a continuous structure throughout the oil, are thought to be largely responsible for the adverse properties of unconventional oils, such as their high viscosity and their high propensity to form emulsions, polymers, and coke. [2]

[1] Kirsten Heimann • Obulisamy Parthiba Karthikeyan Subramanian Senthilkannan Muthu: Biodegradation and Bioconversion of Hydrocarbons. Springer Science+Business Media Singapore 2017. P 339: 340

6.4. Difficulties Associated with the Use of Unconventional Oils

The extraction, transportation and processing of unconventional crude oils are more difficult when compared with light and medium oils, and require the application of special and expensive technologies.

Unconventional oils are often trapped in highly heterogeneous, difficult to extract deposits, and are usually tightly bound to the porous spaces of the reservoir matrix. Furthermore, their high density and viscosity (due to the presence of high concentrations of heavy constituents such as resins and asphaltenes), makes their flow extremely difficult, if not impossible, and can cause the blockage of crude oil extraction equipment. Therefore, the recovery of unconventional crude oils is a challenging and expensive process. [1]

There are two main methods that are used to recover unconventional crude oils. The first one includes non-thermal techniques, where

[2] Kirsten Heimann • Obulisamy Parthiba Karthikeyan Subramanian Senthilkannan Muthu: Biodegradation and Bioconversion of Hydrocarbons. Springer Science+Business Media Singapore 2017. P 340

[1] Kirsten Heimann • Obulisamy Parthiba Karthikeyan Subramanian Senthilkannan Muthu: Biodegradation and Bioconversion of Hydrocarbons. Springer Science+Business Media Singapore 2017. P 342

water, gases, chemicals or mechanical methods are used to release the oil from the substrate. They include water flooding, gas injection, alkaline flooding, polymer flooding, solvent injection, hydraulic fracturing or surface mining, among others. The second approach is thermal production, which includes the injection of hot fluids or steam into the reservoir, as well as in situ combustion. These techniques increase the temperature of the oil, allowing its flow to the production wells through the use of mechanical pumps or gas lift. [1]

6.5. Oil Shale

Two German chemists, Franz Fischer and Hans Tropsch, developed early methods of extracting liquids from coal. The technology involves gasifying coal at high temperature and pressure, and applying catalysts, but there are various different procedures. The process was developed in Germany during the Second World War, and later used in South Africa, when it was subject to an oil embargo. It was sufficient to provide about 30% of that country's needs.

The so-called Oil Shales are immature normal source rocks that have not been heated enough in Nature to give up their hydrocarbons.

---

[1]Kirsten Heimann • Obulisamy Parthiba Karthikeyan Subramanian Senthilkannan Muthu: Biodegradation and Bioconversion of Hydrocarbons. Springer Science+Business Media Singapore 2017. P 342

Strictly speaking they are not shales at all in a geological sense, their scientific name being *kukersite*. They were first exploited in Scotland around 1860, which led to one of the earliest refineries to extract lamp-oil. Another early development was in Estonia where they are still used as a fuel for power stations. [1]

Interest in the development of Oil Shale grew rapidly in the aftermath of the Oil Shock of 1980, especially in the United States, which has large deposits in the Green River Basin of Colorado and neighboring States. The traditional method of extraction was simply to excavate the material, and then place it in retorts at 350–1,000 °C: the higher the temperature, the lighter the product. One drawback was the large amount of fi ne-grained toxic ash produced in the process, whose disposal posed environmental problems. Attempts have also been made at in situ retorting with the help of underground combustion, and the injection of hot natural gas. A recent project, developed by Shell in Colorado, involved inserting electric elements, using electricity from a dedicated coal- fi red power station, and cooking the deposit for several years, after which it is expected to deliver production to conventional wells. In addition, it has been necessary to surround the

[1] C.J. Campbell: Campbell's Atlas of Oil and Gas Depletion. Colin J. Campbell and Alexander Wöstmann 2013. P 369

workings with a refrigerated underground *ice-wall* to prevent the escape of the liquids. It sounds as if it will be subject to an extremely low, if not negative, net energy yield. [1]

There are many other large deposits around the world, especially in Russia, China, Australia, Morocco, Zaire, South Africa, Egypt, Argentina, Chile, Uruguay and Brazil. The resource is enormous, perhaps capable of providing as much as three trillion barrels of oil, but so far none has proved commercially viable, despite in some cases Government subsidy.

Of growing importance are the so-called tight reservoirs, known as *Shale Oil* and *Shale Gas*. In essence they consist of beds of sandstone, siltstone or dolomite with very low porosity and permeability lying within source-rock sequences, commonly at relatively shallow depth. Highly deviated boreholes are drilled into them to run parallel with the formation and thereby be in contact with more of the oil-bearing rock.

Liquids, charged with various chemicals, are then injected under high pressure to fracture the rock and cause artificial permeability, which allows the flow of oil and

[1] C.J. Campbell: Campbell's Atlas of Oil and Gas Depletion. Colin J. Campbell and Alexander Wöstmann 2013. P 369

gas from the adjoining source-rocks. The wells are then placed on production and can produce pro fi table amounts of oil and gas in the current high price environment, although subject to relatively rapid depletion. There are some environmental hazards where the reservoirs are at shallow depth, as the liquids used in the fracturing process may poison the overlying aquifers or cause minor earth tremors. Interest in this new source of oil and gas has expanded rapidly in recent years, especially in the United States, where, the Barnet and Bakken Shales are of particular interest. The environmental hazards have raised objections to developments in several other countries. Obviously, there is a wide range of geological circumstances with the more favorable being exploited first. [1]

Oil can be produced from some organic-rich fine-grained rocks that are normally referred to as "shales" even if the host rock is not strictly a shale by a geologic definition. Production from such sources has a long history. Production of oil from shales for illumination preceded the discovery of conventional petroleum resources in the mid-nineteenth century but for most of the twentieth century production of such oil was a very minor component of global petroleum production.

---

[1] C.J. Campbell: Campbell's Atlas of Oil and Gas Depletion. Colin J. Campbell and Alexander Wöstmann 2013. P 369: 370

However, in the first decade of the twenty-first century there has been a resurgence of interest in these resources because of advances in technology and rising energy prices.

"Oil shales" are rocks that contain significant amounts of solid organic chemical compounds (kerogen) that have not been buried deeply enough to allow for oil maturation. Production is generally done by mining the rock and heating it in a retort in a processing plant close to the mine where the oil and associated gases can be captured. The oil may also be extracted using in situ methods which require heating the subsurface rock by injection of hot fluids, gases, or steam, or by the use of heating elements. As the oil is expelled from the kerogen it can then be induced to flow toward conventional oil wells for extraction.

The leading producer of oil shale in the world is Estonia, where 90% of the power is generated from that source. By far the largest accumulations of oil shale, however, are in the United States, particularly in the Green River Formation of Colorado, Utah, and Wyoming, that were deposited within ancient saline lake systems some 40–50 million years ago. There are also major accumulations in Devonian–Mississippian black shales in the eastern United States that were deposited in marine environments over 350 million years ago. With the high oil prices of the late 1970s a number of pilot projects produced oil from the Green River Formation in Colorado but plans for major commercial exploitation were abandoned when prices fell in the early 1980s. Interest in the potential for production has been rekindled with the high oil prices in recent years. Other countries with significant oil shale accumulations include Australia, Brazil, the Democratic Republic of the Congo, and Russia.

"Shale oil" is oil that is trapped within a fine-grained rock. Extraction of the oil does not require heating but the low permeability of the rocks requires that the rock be artificially fractured in situ to allow flow toward a well. Once regarded only of scientific interest, recent advances in hydraulic fracturing have made shale oil economically viable in some areas. The best-known shale oil accumulation is the Bakken Formation of the Williston Basin of Montana and North Dakota and adjoining parts of Canada. From a geologic perspective, the Bakken is a petroleum source rock that reached maturation but, unlike most mature source rocks, the oil was never expelled to migrate to conventional traps. [1]

---

[1]Ripudaman Malhotra: Fossil Energy. Springer Science+Business Media New York 2013. P 16: 17

6.5.1. Oil Shale Classification

Oil shale can be defined as a sedimentary rock containing various amounts of solid organic material dispersedly bound in a mineral matrix. Oil shales from different deposits vary in their mineral contents and types, chemical composition of organic matter, geological period of deposition, depositional condition, etc. Therefore, there are a number of definitions of oil shale based upon application, operational, or scientific point of view. Similarly, there are various oil shale classification schemes. Moreover, the term "oil shale" is itself somewhat misleading as the organic matter is not oil-like and the mineral matter is not always classifiable as shale.

Following are some selected definitions of oil shale, proposed by several authors in the connection with its energy production or other technological utilization:

1. Gavin defined oil shale as a "compact laminated rock of sedimentary origin, yielding over 33% of ash and containing organic matter that yields oil when distilled, but not appreciably when extracted with ordinary solvents for petroleum."

2. Ozerov and Polozov have described oil shale as "a hard-foliated combustible rock formed by joint accumulation of pelagic plants and animals and mineral mass which had been transformed

by the action of geographic conditions and chemical, biochemical and hydro-chemical processes".

3. Schlatter has characterized oil shale as "a heterogeneous mixture of organic and mineral matter. It is a fine-grained, tight rock with essentially no permeability or porosity".

It is important to note that in defining oil shale for energy-technological purposes, the following oil shale characteristics have been emphasized:

• A high mineral matter content, which may be about two to five times higher than the organic matter content (generally significantly higher in comparison to coals, which contain mineral matter, by definition, of less than 40%).

• The major portion of oil shale organic matter is insoluble in organic solvents (this in contrast to tar sands).

• The organic matter has hydrogen/carbon atomic ratios typically in the range 1.2–1.6 (which is significantly enriched in hydrogen compared with coals, but hydrogen deficient relative to crude oil).

• The capacity of oil shales to ignite and burn without separation of the organic matter from the mineral matter.

- They undergo thermal decomposition that results in production of a significant amount of liquid organic product or shale oil (higher grade oil shales can yield 100 L or more per ton of dry oil shale).

- They have a moisture content of less than 10–13%.

- They exhibit a low permeability of the rock to gases, vapors, and oils.

The organic matter (often termed kerogen; see below) content of oil shale varies widely, ranging typically from 10% to 40%. As the organic matter of oil shale is the source of energy and/or synthetic fuels value, there have been several attempts to classify oil shale by minimum and maximum organic matter content. The upper limit of organic matter content has been proposed to be about 50%, or even higher. The lower organic matter limit is usually defined in relation to the minimum energy requirement of oil shale as an industrial raw material. For example, a lower limit of 5% of organic matter has been proposed to define "commercial deposits." This is because the organic matter content of an oil shale should be at least roughly about 2.5 wt% for the latter to provide the calorific requirements necessary to heat the rock to 500 C.

Oil shale grade or energy potential is currently classified or characterized for commercial purposes on either a heating value or an average oil yield basis.

1. The heating value is used to evaluate the quality of an oil shale in the context of direct firing of oil shale in a power plant to produce heat, commonly used to raise steam for electricity generation. The heating value of typical oil shale kerogen is about 40 MJ/kg. For example, the heating value of an Estonian kuker site oil shale kerogen has been reported to be 37.3 MJ/kg, while for US Green River formation kerogen the value is around 41.1 MJ/kg and for eastern US Devonian kerogen around 37.5 MJ/kg. This is, of course, not the same as the heating value of the oil shale as would be determined for the whole rock, using a standard calorimeter (in which the dilution effect of the zero, or negative, heating value mineral matter is important). A combustion grade oil shale is defined as that having a minimum upper caloric value (for the whole oil shale rock) of 3.1 MJ/kg (dry basis), though a heating value limit of not less than about 4.2–6.3 MJ/kg has been suggested for practical purposes.

2. Average oil yield, or oil production potential, is determined using a "modified" Fischer assay method (the most widely used standardized technique, ASTM D- 3904-80) or an equivalent analytical technique in which the shale is subjected to heating in order to liberate oil from the kerogen. The oil yield depends mostly on

kerogen per mass of oil shale, but may also depend upon the fraction of kerogen convertible to oil (there are differences between different kerogens). On the basis of this assay, an "oil shale" is a shale that yields at least 42 L/t of dry shale (or 10 US gal/t, the basis used by the US Geological Survey), though a limit as low as 25 L/t has also been suggested. Similarly, a crude dividing line between lower and higher-grade shale has been defined at about 100 L of oil/t of shale (with those yielding below 90 L/t considered "low grade," 90–150 L/t "moderate grade," and those above 150 L/t "high grade". Commercial grade oil shales range from about 100–200 L/t of shale. However, the Fischer assay does not actually indicate the maximum oil yield that can be actually produced by a given oil shale. Yields greater than Fischer assay have been obtained by hydro pyrolysis, donor solvents, and rapid heating, especially for lower oil yield, non-softening oil shales.

More than 600 oil shale deposits have been discovered around the world. Oil shales are found in many countries around the world, with nearly 100 major deposits in 27 countries. There exist many surveys/reviews on history of oil shale development throughout the world.

Oil shale resources are typically expressed in either of two different ways: (1) as tons of oil shale, and (2) as crude-shale-oil equivalents contained in the oil shale.

Global deposits have been estimated to be about 411 metric gigatons or to range from 2.8 to 3.3 trillion barrels (4.5 10^{11} to 5.2 10^{11} m^3) of recoverable oil equivalent.

When talking about known oil shale deposits, there is a need to distinguish between two terms – "resources" and "reserves." Resources typically refer to estimates of all deposits of oil shales, while reserves refer only to those from which oil extraction can be economically profitable with the use of existing technologies. It should be noted that these technologies are constantly developing, and because of that, estimates of reserves will not necessarily remain constant over time, irrespective of use or discovery of new resources. [1]

6.5.2. Availability of light tight (shale) oil

The future production of light tight oil by hydraulic fracturing ('fracking') is usually discussed (at least in Europe) in terms of public acceptability relating to water pollution, seismic shocks and greenhouse gas emissions. But generally overlooked is the fact that the total amount of light tight oil (as opposed to tight gas) assessed as globally recoverable is not very large.

---
[1] Ripudaman Malhotra: Fossil Energy. Springer Science+Business Media New York 2013. P 102: 104

from the US EIA (2013) give a somewhat higher estimate, of 345 Gb. Thus, if a 'mid-point' rule is applied to the EIA data, light tight oil can only shift the date of the global 'all-oil' peak by about 5 years, whereas shale gas might potentially shift the 'all-gas' peak by 30 years. While such a calculation is only indicative ('mid-point' not being applicable to non-conventional oils, and 'years of supply' being usually misleading!), it does highlight the relatively small quantity of this type of oil.

6.6. Tight Gas (or Shale Gas)

In conventional fields gas moves easily through the permeable host rock and naturally moves toward wells and up to the surface because of pressure differences. By contrast, sandstones that have very low permeability require considerably more effort to produce the gas. These sandstones are generally thinner than those in conventional fields and have been buried to great depth. The pores in the sandstone, in which the gas is trapped, have been reduced in size by compaction and cementation during burial. These "tight sands" typically occur near the center of sedimentary basins and are sometimes referred to as "basin-centered gas" accumulations. Production of gas from tight sands requires extensive and complex drilling. Because each well produces relatively small volumes of natural gas, many wells must be drilled. Hydraulic fracturing of the host rock can increase the rate of flow of gas to a well.

Although basin-centered gas accumulations can occur over very wide geographic areas, production is generally from limited regions of a basin. The geologic nature of these so-called "sweet spots" is debated as to whether they are regions with enhanced permeability created by natural fractures in the rock or are buoyancy traps similar to conventional gas fields. Resource estimates of basin-centered gas are typically very large but, in some cases, may be reevaluated as geologists develop a better understanding of the nature of sweet spots. Nevertheless, tight gas is undoubtedly a major resource and, historically, it has been the most important component of unconventional gas production in North America but relatively few tight gas fields have yet been developed outside of North America. Production has risen from 10% of total natural gas production in the United States in 1990 to 28% in 2009. Given the magnitude and widespread nature of these accumulations in North America it seems likely that tight gas resources occur in many sedimentary basins worldwide. Exploration and development of such resources must compete with conventional gas resources that are much cheaper to produce, and which in many cases may lie at shallower depths within the same sedimentary basin.

However, it is probably only a matter of time before tight gas resources are developed in many regions of the world. [1]

Shale gas is natural gas with a composition of methane as the main ingredient, which is a found trapped in the source rock which it was formed originally with very fine grains, of very low permeability which makes it difficult to be extracted and its extension can be as large as half of France. It is said to be unconventional because the resource has to be stimulated to enable hydrocarbons to flow due to low permeability, by injecting water at a high pressure to push gas from the rock shale. It is different from the conventional gas which flows into a conventionally drilled well without stimulation giving in large quantities of economic gas.

Horizontal drilling and high-volume hydraulic fracturing (HVHF) are the two advanced technological processes that are used in extracting gas from its shale. Drilling using these techniques can drill a 2-km-deep well and 3 km or more horizontally. These techniques have been extensively used over the last 60 years and known as fracking or hydraulic fracturing. Other types of unconventional gas are tight gas and coalbed methane, aka coal seam gas. These

[1] Ripudaman Malhotra: Fossil Energy. Springer Science+Business Media New York 2013. P 14: 15

advanced technologies have made it possible to extract shale gas in large quantities.

Natural gas combustion releases lower levels of carbon dioxide as well as (CO_2) and Sulphur dioxide than other hydrocarbons such as oil and coal. When used in efficient combined cycle power plants, natural gas combustion can emit less than half as much CO_2 as coal combustion, per unit of electricity output. However, SG extraction has its own technical and environmental impacts. There are currently controversies surrounding the shale gas extraction development in the EU, some advocating for a moratorium because of its negative impacts on human health and environment whilst others see it as a means to boost their nations' energy mix, cheaper and a secure energy source supply. [1]

Certain impermeable carbonaceous rocks may hold substantial amounts of gas, held in the constricted pore space. In some cases, natural fractures allow the gas to seep through the rock, and it can also move along any thin stringers of interbedded permeable sands that are present, forming conduits to conventional wells. Artificial fracturing can also be performed to help extract the gas. The gas content ranges

[1] Joseph Tawonezvi: The legal and regulatory framework for the EU' shale gas exploration and production regulating public health and environmental impacts. Energ. Ecol. Environ. 2017. P 4: 5

widely from, for example, about 5–10 Gcf per square mile in the Appalachian Basin to as much 35 Gcf in the Fort Worth Basin, where it is currently receiving much attention in the so-called Barnet shale play. It is of course very difficult to assess the resource base, but the world total might amount to about 4,000 Tcf. Again, development is most advanced in the United States where some 20,000 wells are producing from such deposits, albeit at low rates. The resource in the ground is large, but production is subject to low net energy yield, high operating costs and environmental hazards, which probably means that the contribution to global supply will remain insignificant for many years to come. The EIA estimates that production of these non-conventional gases in the United States will rise from about 10 Tcf/a in 2010 to as much as 17 Tcf by 2030. No doubt there will be comparable developments in many other countries. But it is early days to evaluate the real potential. As already mentioned there are some environmental objections as the fracking can cause minor earthquakes and pollute the water supply.

Gas may also occur dissolved in deep brines, due to fact that the solubility of methane increases with pressure. Some such deposits may charge shallower reservoirs. The best-known example is in the depths of the fore-deep of Rockies in the Alberta region of Canada. Again, the resource worldwide is considerable and essentially unquantifiable. [1]

SFs have the potential to reduce the geographical concentration of supply and hence increase the energy security and competitiveness of energy markets, but the extent to which other countries will be able to replicate the US success is not clear. Only the EIA has produced a comprehensive assessment of shale resources outside the US. In its latest evaluation, which dates back to June 2013, it extended the number of plays and regions analyzed compared to its 2011 assessment, and showed that China, Australia, Argentina, Mexico, Canada and Algeria are rich in shale resources and shale oil is also plentiful in the Russian subsoil. Although there is no overall evaluation of the proven reserves outside the US, those technically recoverable from the countries considered are 13 times those in the US for SG and 6 times for LTO.

China and Australia, which have so far promoted the production of other non-conventional gases (mainly coalbed methane), have only recently turned to SG development. China has twice the shale resources of the US and holds the largest share of technically recoverable shale oil. Nonetheless, the deposits

---

[1] C.J. Campbell: Campbell's Atlas of Oil and Gas Depletion. Colin J. Campbell and Alexander Wöstmann 2013. P 374

have been discovered in lands difficult to frack with present technology and moreover many basins are poor in water resources. While Australia is still trying to ascertain its reserves, China is trying to acquire foreign technology by supporting inward foreign direct investments in the sector, requiring joint ventures between foreign and Chinese companies. The first partnership between Shell and the national energy company was signed in 2012 using a production sharing agreement, but has not gone beyond a preliminary exploration stage. Effective production is turning out to be far below the initial expectations: barely 0.2 billion cubic meters were produced in China in 2013, forcing the country to severely downgrade its 2015 targets. The projection for 2015 has been more than halved from the 15 billion cubic meters (less than 1 % of current US production) expected in 2012 to 6.8 bcm. This postponement of the exploitation stage is due to several hurdles, such as a lack of infrastructure and a scarcity of technological and human skills, and more generally to poor business experience. There are also bureaucratic and legal barriers linked to state concessions and to landowner compensation. [1]

---

[1] Rossella Bardazzi • Maria Grazia Pazienza Alberto Tonini: European Energy and Climate Security. Springer International Publishing Switzerland 2016. P 147: 148

Due to its environmental friendliness, natural gas has played a prominent role from the late 20th century. Currently, a large portion of the natural gas comes from unconventional sources (e.g., shale gas, tight gas, coal bed methane, and, soon, gas hydrates). Unconventional gas reservoirs are loosely defined as those that cannot be produced with conventional techniques. It turns out that the volume of gas available increases exponentially as conventional gas moves to unconventional gas. The Figure shows that the endowment of conventional gas is estimated at 15,100 Tcf and that of unconventional gas is estimated at 52,700 Tcf except for gas hydrates. Unconventional natural gas has been more difficult and costly to exploit than conventional deposits, until recently. Among these

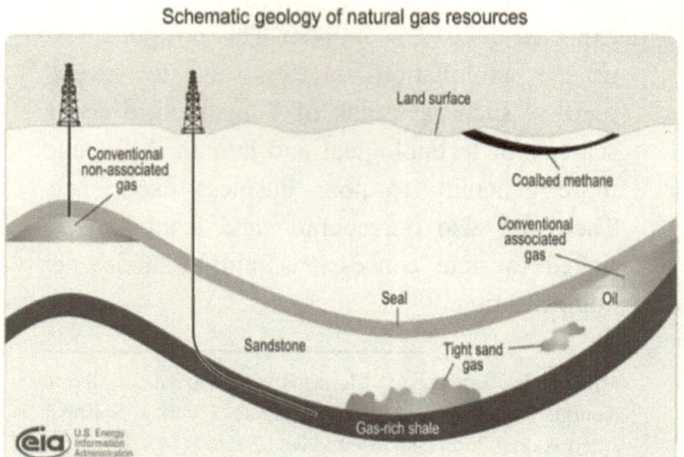

Schematic geology of natural gas resources

unconventional resources, shale and tight gas exploitation are widely commercialized, with constant improvement of fracturing techniques to increase yield and decrease costs.

The Figure shows the geologic nature of most major sources of natural gas in schematic form (EIA 2010). Gas-rich shale is the source rock for many natural gas resources, but, until now, has not been a focus for production. Horizontal drilling and hydraulic fracturing have made shale gas an economically viable alternative to conventional gas resources. Conventional gas accumulations occur when gas migrates from gas rich shale into an overlying sandstone formation, and then becomes trapped by an overlying impermeable formation, called the seal.

Associated gas accumulates in conjunction with oil, while non-associated gas does not accumulate with oil. Tight sand gas accumulations occur in a variety of geologic settings where gas migrates from a source rock into a sandstone formation, but is limited in its ability to migrate upward due to reduced permeability in the sandstone. Coal bed methane does not migrate from shale, but is generated during the transformation of organic material to coal.

The recent boom in natural gas production in the United States, which has been brought through technical innovations in the recovery of natural gas from previously inaccessible shale rock formations, has helped lower electricity costs and benefitted the petrochemical and manufacturing industries. Even more significantly, it has contributed to a drop in United States carbon dioxide emissions. EIA report (2013b) shows that energy-related carbon dioxide emissions are at their lowest level since 1994 and have fallen 12 % between 2007 and 2012. As a result, inexpensive natural gas accelerates the closure of aging coal plants around the country.

Shale gas formations are usually mature petroleum source rocks where high levels of heat and pressure have converted the source rock material to natural gas.

Characteristics of shale gas reservoirs are different from those of typical conventional reservoirs. Shale is a fissile mudstone consisting of silt, 4 * 60 μm, and clay-size particles, less than 4 μm, which are largely mineral fragments. Shale is characterized by thin, parallel, horizontal layers which are formed as cumulative deposits of sedimentary rock (sand, silt, mud, decaying plants and animals and other microorganisms) compressed over long periods of time (millions of years), a process known as compaction. Shale hydrocarbon reservoirs, in addition to mineral fragments, include a small amount of organic matter. Organic material is transformed into hydrocarbon under large overburden stress and high temperature conditions. It also creates a large internal hydrostatic pressure locally, which could cause creation of micro-fracture pores because of the fluid expansion force. The pore size in shale could be less than 2 nm or as high as 2 μm. Nanopores create large capillary pressures, lower the critical pressure, and temperature of hydrocarbon components creating a shift in the phase envelope of the resident fluids, and cause capillary condensation and slippage of gas molecules at the pore walls (Knudsen flow). Because of low matrix permeability, Darcy flow (advection) becomes so small that molecular diffusion can play a significant role in the mass transfer of fluids from the matrix to micro and macro fractures. Hydrocarbon-rich shale reservoirs are typically oil wet while their counterparts, tight sandstones, are generally water wet. In shale gas reservoirs, both free gas and adsorbed gas adsorbed exist. Free gas exists in pore spaces of the matrix and natural fractures, and adsorbed gas is stored on the surface of matrix particles and the faces of natural fractures. Several studies presented that gas desorption may contribute 5 * 30 % of total gas production, but this effect is observed at the late time of well production.

Shale reservoirs have very low permeability and porosity. A typical shale reservoir has a very low permeability matrix of about 1 to 100 nd and a porosity of less than 10 %. To exploit ultra-low permeability reservoirs, hydraulic fracturing technology has been proven to be an effective means. Hydraulic fracturing is a process used in nine out of 10 natural gas wells in the United States, where millions of gallons of water, sand and chemicals are pumped underground to break apart the rock and release the gas. The Figure show the process of hydraulic fracturing. Hydraulic fracturing induces fractures with enormously high permeability and makes fracture networks of interconnected fractures around the wellbore.

Since shale gas reservoirs are relatively thin and infinite laterally, horizontal wells are usually applied to improve production by increasing the contact area of wellbore and the pay zone. The great increase of the surface area of the wellbore facilitates that fluids flow freely from the reservoir to the wellbore. To effectively access the reservoir pores, drilling engineers drill long horizontal wells in the formation parallel to the minimum horizontal stress direction. Then, completion engineers place a large set of multistage transverse hydraulic fractures in each well

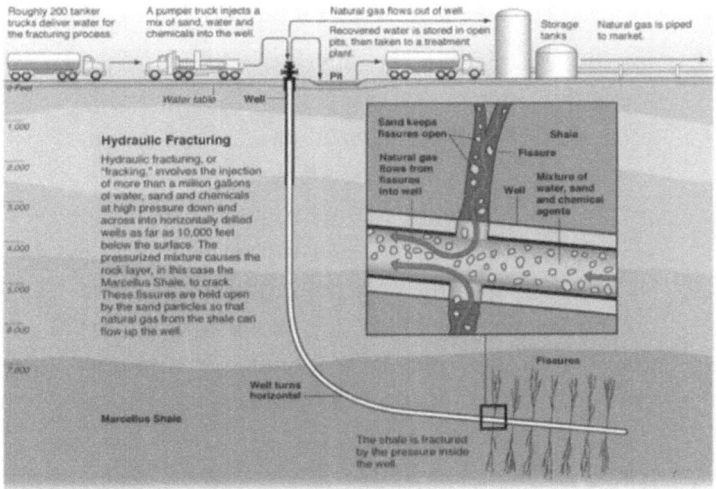

Graphic by Al Granberg

to stimulate the drainage volume of the well. The horizontal well segment is in the range of 4000–10,000 ft in length (5000 ft in Eagle Ford, U.S.A. and 9000 ft in Bakken, U.S.A.), consisting of 20–50 transverse hydraulic fractures in the multistage stimulation process. Each horizontal well is usually from 350 to 1200 ft apart (350 and 700 ft in Eagle Ford and 1200 ft in Bakken). Flow rates in extremely low permeability shale gas reservoirs depend on the total area of permeable fractures that are hydraulically connected to the well and the matrix permeability of the shale formation. The multistage hydraulic fractures create a dual-porosity environment in the wellbore drainage area, called the "stimulated reservoir volume (SRV)." The dual-porosity environment makes it easier for hydrocarbons to flow from small pores of the matrix, to micro and macro fractures, and to the wellbore. The inverse of this flow hierarchy is much less effective in fluid injection processes. To confirm the dual-porosity nature of the SRV, reservoir engineers compare the permeability from the rate transient test with that of the cores. If the transient-test permeability is much larger than the core permeability, it can be concluded that the hydraulic fracturing process has induced macro-fractures, which, in turn, has created a larger formation effective permeability than that of the matrix.

The central geological properties of a shale gas play are generally assessed in terms of organic geochemistry, organic richness, thickness, thermal maturity, and mineralogy. For the successful production in shale gas reservoirs, high total organic carbon (TOC) content and thermal maturity, relevant thickness, and a low clay content/high brittle mineral content are needed. Shale gas organic geochemistry is a function of the depositional environment and is similar to conventional source rock geochemistry. Lacustrine shale, marine shale, and terrestrial/coal bed shale is typically associated with Type I, II, and III kerogens. Target TOC (wt% kerogen) values are somewhat interrelated to the thickness and other factors that influence gas yield. For commercial shale gas production, Rezaee (2015) notes a target TOC of a least 3 %, while Lu et al. (2012) states that a TOC of 2 % is generally regarded as the lower limit of commercial production in the United States. That said, TOC varies considerably throughout any one shale gas play. The thickness of economic gas shale is one of many considerations. As an example, in North America, the effective thicknesses of shale gas pay zones range from 6 m (Fayetteville, U.S.A.) to 304 m (Marcellus, U.S.A.) (Caineng et al. 2010). Caineng et al. (2010) note a guidance thickness for economic plays of 30guidance thickness for economic plays50 m, where development is continuous and the TOC (wt%) is greater than 2 %. TOC is only an indication of shale gas potential. The actual accumulation of gas from the organic compounds within the shale requires the organic matter to first generate the gas and this is function of the thermal maturity.

Significant shale gas is typically only generated beyond vitrinite reflectance (Ro%) values of approximately 0.7 % (Type III kerogen) to 1.1 % (Type I and II kerogen), which corresponds to depth of between 3.5 and 4.2 km. However, the most favorable situation is when virtinite reflectance values range from 1.1 to 1.4. Mineralogy also plays a central role when evaluating gas shale, due to its impact on the performance of fracture treatment. In terms of mineralogy, brittle minerals such as quartz, feldspar, calcite, and dolomite are favorable for the development of extensive fractures throughout the formation in response to fracture treatment. According to Caineng et al. (2010), the brittle mineral content should be greater than 40 % to enable sufficient fracture propagation.

Alternatively, Lu et al. (2012) note that in the main shale gas producing areas of the United States, the brittle mineral content is generally greater than 50 % and the clay content is less than 50 %. In more simplistic terms, high clay content results in a more ductile response to hydraulic fracturing, with the shale deforming instead of shattering.

According to EIA report (2014), by 2035, natural gas surpasses coal as the largest source of United States electricity generation. The report anticipated that the share of electricity generated from natural gas grows steadily so that natural gas plants account for more than 70 % of all new capacity. In this situation, shale gas provides the largest source of growth in United States natural gas supply. The Figure shows the history and prediction of United States natural gas production by source. The 56 % increase in total natural gas production from 2012 to 2040 in the reference case results from increased development of shale gas, tight gas, and offshore natural gas resources. Shale gas production is the largest contributor, growing by more than 10 Tcf, from 9.7 Tcf in 2012 to 19.8 Tcf in 2040. The shale

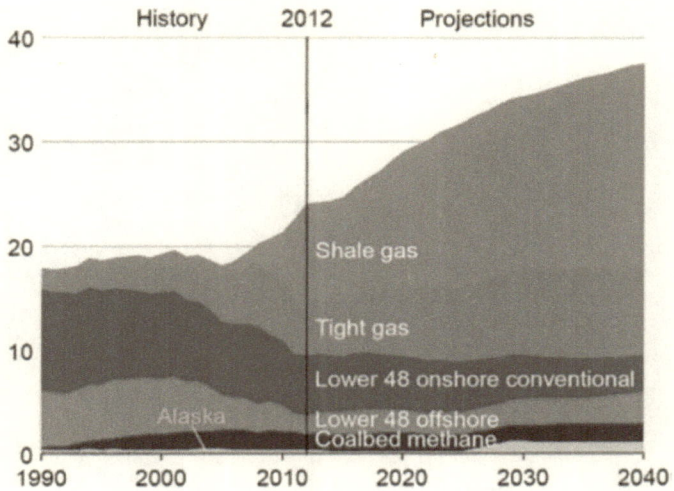

gas share of total United States natural gas production increases from 40 % in 2012 to 53 % in 2040. Tight gas production also increases by 73 % from 2012 to 2040.

The Figure shows the location of shale basins and the regions analyzed. Red colored areas represent the location of basins with shale formations for which estimates of the risked oil and natural gas in-place and technically recoverable resources were provided. Tan colored areas represent the location of basins that were reviewed, but for which shale resource estimates were not provided, mainly due to the lack of data necessary to conduct the assessment. White colored areas were not assessed in the report. The Figure shows that there are 137 shale formations in 41 countries. Estimates of EIA report also provides technically

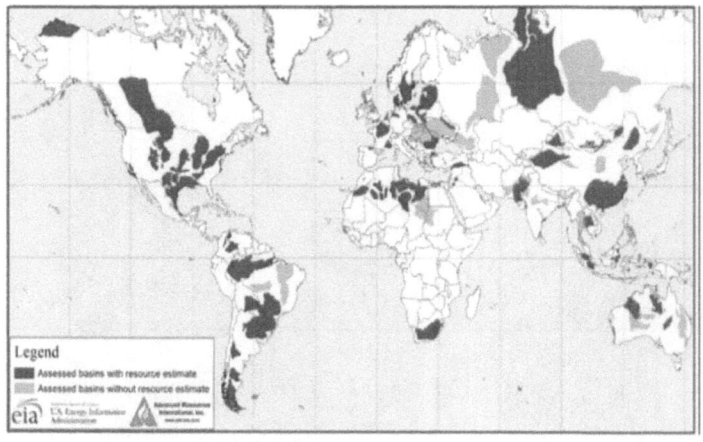

recoverable resources of 345 billion barrels of world shale oil resources and 7299 trillion cubic feet of world shale gas resources (EIA 2013a). The estimates of unproved technically recoverable shale oil and gas resources in country-level detail are presented in Table.

Region totals and selected countries	2013 EIA/ARI unproved wet shale gas technically recoverable resources (TRR)	2013 EIA/ARI unproved shale oil technically recoverable resources (TRR)
Europe	470	12,900
Bulgaria	17	200
Denmark	32	0
France	137	4700
Germany	17	700
Netherlands	26	2900
Norway	0	0
Poland	148	3300
Romania	51	300
Spain	8	100
Sweden	10	0
United Kingdom	26	700
Former Soviet Union	415	77,200
Lithuania	0	300
Russia	287	75,800
Ukraine	128	1100
North America	1685	80,000
Canada	573	8800
Mexico	545	13,100
United States	567	58,100
Asia and Pacific	1607	61,000
Australia	437	17,500
China	1115	32,200
Indonesia	46	7900
Mongolia	4	3400
Thailand	5	0
South Asia	201	12,900
India	96	3800
Pakistan	105	9100
Middle East and North Africa	1003	42,900

Region totals and selected countries	2013 EIA/ARI unproved wet shale gas technically recoverable resources (TRR)	2013 EIA/ARI unproved shale oil technically recoverable resources (TRR)
Algeria	707	5700
Egypt	100	4600
Jordan	7	100
Libya	122	26,100
Morocco	12	0
Tunisia	23	1500
Turkey	24	4700
Western Sahara	8	200
Sub-Saharan Africa	390	100
Mauritania	0	100
South Africa	390	0
South America and Caribbean	1430	59,700
Argentina	802	27,000
Bolivia	36	600
Brazil	245	5300
Chile	48	2300
Colombia	55	6800
Paraguay	75	3700
Uruguay	2	600
Venezuela	167	13,400
Total world	7201	345,000

The possibility of cheaper and cleaner energy from shale gas has prompted interest from governments around the world. If it can achieve the necessary innovations for tapping perhaps the largest shale gas reserves in the world, China may be able to reduce its dependence on coal and shift to a lower-carbon economy. European countries such as the United Kingdom are also exploring the possibility of exploiting shale gas However, caution is warranted. The large deployment of fracking technology faces significant hurdles outside of the United States context. China's nascent industry is plagued by technical bottlenecks, lack of adequate water supply, and poor infrastructure. Drilling an exploratory shale gas well in China still costs much more than it does in the United States. In Europe, the challenges are more likely to be political and legal. Unlike in the United States, European landowners do not automatically own the rights to extract the resources from the ground beneath their property, making the building of new extraction plants fraught with political difficulties Shale gas therefore has the potential to be very significant source of natural gas, and has the potential to greatly increase the gas resource of many nations across the globe. As outlined by Ridley (2011), the significance and future of shale gas will be influenced by the interplay of a wide variety of other issues, including the following:

potentially falling gas prices due to increased production, increased demand for gas due to increased adoption of natural gas to produce energy, and reduced production costs due to technological development. Among these, for the understanding of shale gas reservoir, this book provides comprehensive technical

[1]Kun Sang Lee • Tae Hong Kim: Integrative Understanding of Shale Gas Reservoirs. 2016. P 3: 11

information in terms of petroleum reservoir engineering. [1]

Carbon capture and storage to mitigate the impact of CO_2 emissions from the power and industrial sectors receives increased interest in importance, and sequestration of CO_2 in gas shale formations has significant potential. Shales are widely distributed. Fracked shales have infrastructure in place that can be used for CO_2 storage. The CO_2 storage in shale formations has reduced potential for induced seismicity relative to CO_2 storage in saline aquifers. Furthermore, EGR using CO_2 presents an interesting opportunity to produce a relatively clean burning fuel while simultaneously promoting environmental sustainability through CO_2 storage. We recognize, however, that various studies suggest that shale gas production and utilization may result in significant GHG emissions depending on the total fugitive CH_4 emissions during extraction and utilization. Additionally, extraction of shale gas may have negative impacts on water resources, public health, biodiversity, food supply and soil without adequate technical precautions and regulatory oversight. Hence, EGR and storage of CO_2 in gas shale formations must be further explored before the environmental benefits can be decisively concluded.

technically recoverable shale gas is abundant globally although only the United

States and Canada have made substantial progress in the development and production of shale gas reservoirs. Several countries with substantial technically recoverable shale gas, such as China and countries in the MENA region, are struggling not only with technical challenges for shale gas development, but also financial and regulatory challenges. Nonetheless, there is a great global opportunity for developing large, economically recoverable shale gas resources, and so it is necessary to investigate now how such reservoirs may perform for both CO_2 storage and EGR. Our review of the literature on this topic suggests that CO_2 storage and EGR are viable, yet dependent on shale physical characteristics. Hence, knowledge of shale properties is critical to assessing the economic viability of CO_2 storage in shales.

shales are in fact a good medium for CO_2 storage with capacities of 5–10 kg/ton of formation or approximately 1 million metric tons per square kilometer. This level of storage capacity suggests a substantial opportunity for CO_2 storage in shales. The opportunity for CO_2 storage in shales via EGR becomes even more attractive as significant energy can be extracted with relatively modest energy input. As discussed in this chapter, EGR can be used to exploit the high affinity of shales for $CO2$ relative to CH_4 (14:1 on a mass basis).

Although widespread exploitation of shale gas resources and the long-term economic viability of carbon capture and storage are not certain, the state of knowledge regarding geologic storage of CO_2 and EGR in shale formations needs to be improved in order to make these processes viable as the extraction of gas from shale resources gains traction globally. there is a very good opportunity globally regarding the future of geologic storage of CO_2 in depleted shale gas formations and as part of EGR operations. [1]

6.7. Energy return on energy invested

Energy return on energy invested ('EROEI', or 'EROI') is a significant issue, but one not receiving attention in nearly all global oil models (and not in the mainstream 'all-energy' models, for that matter). The data are probably still not adequate to give a comprehensive picture, but none the less are sobering, as shown in Table.

The recently rapidly falling EROI ratio for conventional oil, if confirmed by other studies, is of concern as independently Hall and co-workers have suggested that modern society

[1] Roozbeh Khosrokhavar: Mechanisms for CO2 Sequestration in Geological Formations and Enhanced Gas Recovery. Doctoral Thesis. Springer International Publishing Switzerland 2016. P 90: 91

needs a minimum EROI ratio of perhaps 10–15:1 from its fuel sources to function in its current form (e.g. Hall 2008; Lambert et al. 2014). And even where EROI ratios are higher than this, being lower than in the past reduces society's overall wealth if not compensated for by productivity or efficiency gains elsewhere.

Recently, Campbell (2015) has incorporated EROI ratios into his global oil forecast, multiplying his forecast production levels for the various categories of oil

Table 3.2 Approximate ranges for EROI ratios

Conventional oil	Date: 1920	1970	1995	2006	2012
US	20	30	35	20	10
Global publicly traded			36	18	
Other energies					
Tar sands	1.5–8				
Coal	40–80				
Nuclear fission	4–16			(N.B. Old data, possibly out of date)	
Wind	10–28				
PV	2.5–8				
Biodiesel, gasohol	~3				

('Regular conventional', Deepwater, tar sands, etc.) by the corresponding 'net yield' ratio to turn gross barrels of production by category of oil into a corresponding forecast of 'net-energy' barrels. Because the non-conventional oils have—in general— lower EROI ratios than conventional oil, the overall decline in global production is steeper in net-barrels terms than in gross barrels.

And in terms of investment required to produce future oil, as mentioned earlier note that the need for increasing quantities of a resource to extract that resource was one of the drivers of system collapse in the original Limits to Growth modelling (the other driver being rising costs from increasing pollution).

Finally, an often-overlooked aspect of EROI data is net-energy rate limits. These are limits to the maximum rate that an energy-producing technology (in this case, a new fuel source) can be usefully introduced, and reflect the fact that if the technology is introduced faster than the embodied energy required for new plant, the overall net-energy yield during the growth phase is negative. (For example, photovoltaics, with about 200 GWp installed, have to date yielded no net-energy to mankind. This is partly due to having a moderate EROI ratio, but mainly to their rapid uptake, And even where technology is introduced at a slower pace, the net-energy yield can be significantly less than the energy yield as usually calculated. Most current global energy models do not take into account either EROI ratios or net-energy rate limits. [1]

A major cause of confusion in oil statistics is that there is no standard definition of

[1] R.W. Bentley: Introduction to Peak Oil. Springer International Publishing Switzerland 2016. P 67: 69

the boundary between the so-called *Conventional* and *Unconventional* oil and gas. It is clearly important to make clear distinctions because the different categories have different distributions, rates of extraction, costs and other characteristics. In this study, it has been found expedient to recognize what is termed *Regular Conventional Oil (>17.5 o API)* and *Gas*, defined to exclude the following categories, which are designated as *Non-Conventional:*

1. Oil from coal and organic-rich clays *(kukersite)*, commonly termed *oil shale*

2. Oil extracted by the artificial fracturing of low permeability reservoirs (Shale *Oil* or *Tight Oil)*

3. Extra-Heavy Oil (<10 o API) and bitumen

4. Heavy Oil (10–17.5 o API)

5. Deepwater Oil and Gas (>500 m water depth)

6. Polar Oil and Gas

7. Liquids from gas plants

8. Gas from coal (coalbed methane), tight reservoirs (shale *gas)*, deep brines and hydrates. (Note: °API is a measure of density, with water having a density of 10 API)

The resources of *Non-Conventional Oil and Gas* are large, but extraction is normally difficult, costly, environmentally damaging and, above all, slow. The entry of supply from these sources in the future is clearly important, serving to ameliorate the post-peak decline, but it is doubted if they will have much impact on the date or height of the overall peak itself. They are described briefly below. [1]

A conventional reservoir is naturally pressurized, or more commonly, over-pressurized for the formation pressure of a hydrocarbon-free sediment at the same depth and geological situation. Conventional gas deposits will flow spontaneously to the surface when a reservoir is drilled, and the risk of blowout venting is pervasive in all conventional hydrocarbons, particularly those found at greater depths and higher pressures.

In contrast, an unconventional deposit is one that must be stimulated in some way in order to cause the hydrocarbon to flow. In a conventional gas deposit these processes (steam or hot water injection, chemical solvent injection, gas injection, etc.) would be considered to be a secondary recovery technique that are applied to recover hydrocarbons that would otherwise have to be left in the reservoir.

NGH is one of a number of unconventional gas plays that is essentially

---

[1] C.J. Campbell: Campbell's Atlas of Oil and Gas Depletion. Colin J. Campbell and Alexander Wöstmann 2013. P 369

stable within its reservoir. The physical conditions of unconventional gas plays must be altered in some way to allow the natural gas to be produced. In the case of coalbed methane, water is pumped out of the gas-infused coal-shale measures, resulting in the release of largely dissolved gas. In the case of shale gas and tight gas sands, permeability has to be induced by fracking. In the case of NGH, the physical conditions affecting its stability field have to be altered so that the NGH converts to its gas and water components. Either or both pressure or temperature can be altered to achieve the conversion. In addition, conversion can be induced through a controlled dissolution process and molecular substitution.

NGH exists in a very different way to other gas deposits. Conventional gas and the other unconventional gas deposits are related to geological traps in which they may have resided for hundreds of millions of years. The other unconventional gas deposits also have considerable geological permanence.

In contrast, oceanic NGH resides in an existing thermodynamic or physical/ chemical 'trap' that is strongly influenced by changing environmental conditions.

Natural gas in solid NGH is the result of a crystallization process driven by the mineralizing solutions within the GHSZ. In fact, type 2 concentrations may occur in an open pore water situation in which subjacent water passes through the NGH-enriched zone and may vent to the seafloor. If the water media in contact with the NGH ceased having sufficient gas concentration, the NGH would dissolve into the water to maintain diffusional balance.

Perhaps the principle reason why there is wide interest in NGH is that there appears to be huge volumes of natural gas sequestered in NGH, and large concentrations have been identified. Estimates of natural gas in NGH indicate that the resource base may be of greater volume than is estimated to be in conventional gas deposits. In order to optimize exploration for oceanic NGH, however, it is important to understand the paragenesis and geological model for concentrated NGH, so that exploration can be focused upon them. NGH occurs in permafrost regions and in oceanic marine sediments in deep continental shelves and margins. [1]

---

[1] Michael D. Max · Arthur H. Johnson William P. Dillon: Natural Gas Hydrate – Arctic Ocean Deepwater Resource Potential. 2013. P 25: 26

7. Peak of the Global Production of 'All-Oil', and 'All-Liquids'

So now we must turn from examining the date of peak of global conventional oil production to the peak for the global production of all-oil; and also, that of all liquids, where the latter includes GTLs, CTLs and biofuels.

Here a key point from the IEA data is that as the global peak of conventional oil production approaches, and hence the scope for increases from its production starts to tail off, the world is forced to use increasing volumes of the non-conventional sources to satisfy any increase in demand. And since, as indicated in the Figure, these sources are generally more expensive to produce than conventional oil, the overall oil price is expected to rise to the level of the marginal barrel required. As mentioned earlier, this marginal-barrel price is currently roughly around $100/bbl, although the highest IHS-CERA value given in the Miller and Sorrell (2014) paper quoted earlier is $160/bbl for 'Canada oil sand mine upgraded' oil assuming a 15 % rate of return.

At some later date, once the peak of global conventional oil production is past and the decline in the production of this oil has settled in, modelling shows that global production of this oil is likely to fall at between about 2 and 3 % annually.

This figure reflects an average decline of around 5 % annually from post-peak fields being partially offset by increasing production from late fields coming on-stream.

A 2–3 % decline in conventional oil represents an annual loss of global production of about 1.5–2.0 Mb/d; i.e., a decade's decline will give a loss of around 15 Mb/d.

If the extra supply from the non-conventional oils and other liquids is not enough to offset this loss, and meet potential rising demand in addition, then global 'oil shocks' are inevitable unless demand for oil is curtailed by other factors.

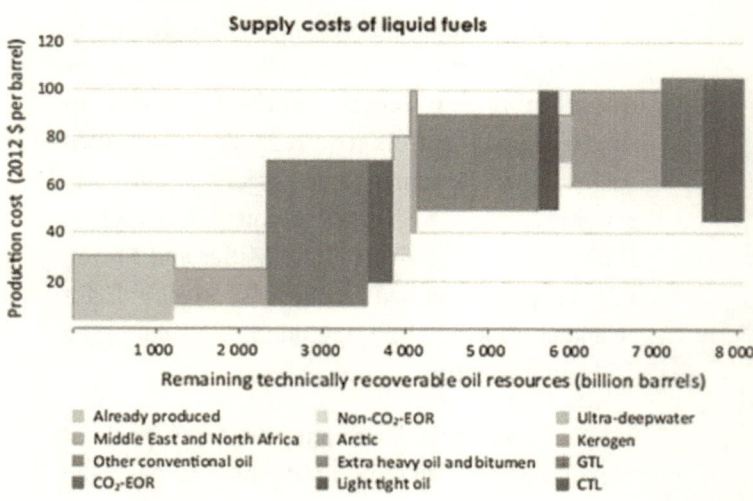

7.1. Global Estimates

Inputs of oil to the marine and coastal environment arise from a wide variety of sources, and all may make significant contributions. Releases of crude oil and refined products from a range of both non-point source (NPS) and point sources cause acute and chronic pollution in rivers, surface and ground waters, coastal and marine areas. Hydrocarbons are introduced directly into sedimentary environments from a variety of anthropogenic activities along urban waterways (e.g. petroleum terminals and refineries, power stations, aluminum smelters, gas production facilities, tar distillation plants, railway sidings, loading/unloading facilities, shipyards, breaking yards, waste management facilities, marinas, and residential areas). Petroleum and coal- or oil-derived tars are also point sources arising from natural seeps as well as from spills. [1]

7.2. Oil Forecasts Prior to 1956

Peak oil sceptics point out the incorrect forecasts over many years for either the US or global peaks of conventional oil production. This view has some validity. Oil has long been a vital resource, and it is only natural that people

[1] Kirsten Heimann • Obulisamy Parthiba Karthikeyan Subramanian Senthilkannan Muthu: Biodegradation and Bioconversion of Hydrocarbons. Springer Science+Business Media Singapore 2017. P 11

have questioned its future availability on the basis of information available at the time.

Forecasts for the US made prior to the discovery of the East Texas field in the US in 1930, and the subsequent peak of US discoveries in new fields in the mid-1930s, were always likely to be underestimates. Likewise, forecasts for the world as a whole prior to the discovery of Ghawar in Saudi Arabia in 1948, and the subsequent peak of global discoveries of oil in new fields in the mid-1960s, were also likely to underestimate future production. However, once these discovery peaks had been passed, forecasting future production peaks for conventional oil was relatively straightforward, provided good data and correct approaches were used.

For example, when Hubbert made his 1956 prediction of the US Lower-48 conventional oil peak being between 1965 and 1970, discovery of US oil in new fields had been in decline for about 20 years. And for the world, the 'technically-based' forecasts from the mid-1970s to 1980s discussed below, of the global conventional oil peak around the year 2000, were made when global discovery of oil in new fields had been in decline for from one to two decades.

Note that Hubbert's was not the only US or world forecast around these dates, a similar US forecast was made by Pogue and Hill a month earlier than Hubbert; and world oil forecasts made around that period are referenced in National Petroleum Council (2007). [1]

7.3. The Second Half of the Oil Age

Colin Campbell, a noted analyst in the field, calls the new era of global oil supply that we are entering 'The Second half of the Oil Age'. Given that for the century and a half of the 'First half of the Oil Age' the world used primarily conventional oil from oil fields, what would indicate the start of the 'Second half'?

There are several candidates to mark this transition point. Arguably the 'Second half' starts at the point that we are facing now, where the world's ability to increase production of conventional oil becomes insufficient to meet its increasing demand for oil. It is true that currently some of the conventional oil that could come to market is being held back by some suppliers, but taking this constraint into account and also recognizing that most suppliers of conventional oil are now past their 'mid-point peaks' in production, for some years now the world has required increasing production of the non-conventional oils (primarily natural gas liquids, tar sands oils, shale oil from fracking,

[1] R.W. Bentley: Introduction to Peak Oil. Springer International Publishing Switzerland 2016. P 58

and biofuels) to make up for what conventional oil in fields cannot supply. This in turn pushed up the price of oil since 2005 to levels that damaged global economic activity.

A later point for entry into the 'Second half of the Oil Age' is when the global production of conventional oil stops increasing and goes into decline, driven primarily by lack of recoverable resource of this type of oil. At the time of writing (Summer 2015) it is not clear whether this point has been passed—the IEA has perhaps suggested it was passed in 2006—or if it will be some time in the future; the date in part depends on how 'conventional oil' is defined, and also on the extent that oil producers find the application of enhanced oil recovery measures in conventional oil fields to be profitable. But when this point occurs, the increased production from the non-conventional oils must not only be enough to meet increased demand, but also to offset the decline in the production of conventional oil.

This leads to the final point in time where entry to the 'Second half of the Oil Age' becomes apparent. As mentioned, the expected fall in the global production of conventional oil, once past its 'resource-limited' peak, is likely to be of the order of 2–3 % per year. It is not clear that production of the non-conventional oils can take up the slack, nor at what price; and a number of forecasting models suggests that this may not be possible. If this is indeed the case, i.e., if insufficient non-conventional oil production comes forward, then global oil production in total declines, and the 'Second half of the Oil Age' is well and truly here.

For forecasting oil production, so far in this book we have largely relied on the rule of thumb of 'peak at mid-point'. This is an extremely valuable and generally robust approach, but necessarily only a broad approximation. [1]

7.4. Hubbert's Peak

The time of harbingered catastrophes constituted a time of learning, discovery, and experimentation related to the awareness of a civilizational change. Societies were confronted with an epochal shift that represented the dislocation of the core engine of growth from reproducible and universal productive factors toward exhaustible, non-renewable, and unevenly distributed resources. With fossil fuel consumption mounting to unprecedented levels and no clear idea of the remaining stocks underground, there was a growing sense of alarm as to whether the resources might run out in the near future.

---

[1] R.W. Bentley: Introduction to Peak Oil. Springer International Publishing Switzerland 2016. P 53: 55

Ultimately, the pessimism associated with the first forecasts sprang from a determinist conception of human action. Determinist is used here to mean that given an array of initial conditions, no alternative outcomes were feasible. For depletion viewpoints, not only did all factors push toward the same outcome, but the unintended consequences of these factors also did so. Strange though it may seem, the first generation of conservationists did not foresee (or, at least, failed to mention) that, at a certain point, consumption would begin to fall if the price of natural resources began rising. The disregard for every factor that might counteract the lemming-like rush toward "depletion day" set the stage for the realization of a catastrophic outlook. With economic growth, technological innovation, population growth, and social affluence all driving the increase in fossil fuel consumption, the time would be reached when the last non-renewable resource was consumed and spent. The striking point in this conception is that peak production fully coincided with depletion: Fossil fuels would cease to exist precisely when humanity was consuming the most commercial energy. It is this assumption of rising consumption trends through to depletion that is largely responsible for the dramatic, teleological representation of a Doomsday scenario. Central to such a view is the formalization of reserves-to-production ratios(R/P), calculated by dividing the estimate of proven reserves by the current level of production. The result discloses the time remaining before oil becomes completely exhausted, assuming the current level of extraction remains constant. Bluntly interpreted, reserve-to-production ratios become the telltale signs of an impending, unavoidable, threatening deadline.

Notwithstanding the doubts and uncertainties that surrounded the depletion scenario, the engagement of governments, social interests, and scientists in a prolonged public debate contributed to ingraining the idea throughout societies that the valuation of the future entailed choices in the present. And the more extensive the appraisal, the more justified the change. Following the theoretical insights made by other social sciences, we make recourse to the "time discount" concept to assess how people ascribed a present value to the rewards to be received in the future. Somehow, time discounting quite sharply reflects the environmental stand toward conservation and how much people are willing to save or sacrifice their current benefits for the sake of a more balanced future. According to this concept, a high time discount rate means that future rewards hold only a small present value so that a higher discount is placed on potential returns. Low discount rates mean the reverse: A higher appraisal of what is to be collected in the future. Moreover, it is assumed that people may either discount utility according to inter-temporal preferences or set their own discount preferences in line with political and moral values such as intergenerational solidarity or landscape preservation.

As the Fig. demonstrates, the environmental point of view held by conservationists is represented by a dashed line. They perceive access to natural resources as part and parcel of citizenship and that the market should discount future profits at the same rate as society would wish to discount the welfare of future generations.

As these natural resources are not just economic goods but the national heritage of future generations, the closer society comes to "depletion day," the scarcer the asset becomes and the higher its present value should also become. Therefore, the future rewards of present resources tend to evolve in a hyperbolic slope.

The second perspective is that of political economists and is portrayed by the solid line. What distinguishes this strand of thought is its recognition that the current value of fossil fuel resources will tend to increase in line with the approaching date of exhaustion. The reason for the future escalation of prices is the "degradation of costs" provoked by extracting oil (or coal) from deeper, smaller, and thinner reservoirs. Although technological improvements could contribute to slowing this trend, their overall effect is offset by the greater costs inevitably incurred as extraction meets new and more difficult conditions.

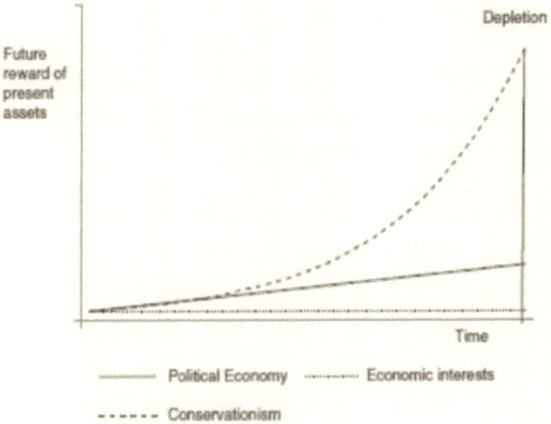

Finally, there is the stance taken by oil explorers, companies, and others involved in the trade and described in the caption to the Fig. as "economic interests."

Altogether, this group had to face the discourse of impending shortage and contend with the sheer inevitability of "D-day." However, it did seem acceptable to believe that future additions to known reserves might extend the depletion gap to unimaginable levels and behave as if "D-day" was completely out of both sight and mind. To underpin this position, they claimed that the present value of rewards should remain unchanged into the future.

The noteworthy point behind the different valuations of the future is that all streams of thought shared the same belief toward the forthcoming time in which the last available non-renewable resource would be spent at the very peak of production.

Fossil fuels were doomed to disappear precisely at the moment when they were most needed: peak meant catastrophe.

It took some decades before the refutation of this thorny perspective emerged. Even nowadays, the idea that total exhaustion coincides with the moment of maximum production sometimes looms in public comments. However, in as early as 1956, an American geophysicist working at the Shell research laboratory, in Houston, made an important contribution that shattered these preconceptions. His name was King Hubbert. According to Hubbert, peak production does not signal the exhaustion of recoverable oil, but rather the reaching of the halfway point on the way to global exhaustion. On the historical time line, the peak indicates that humanity has extracted half of the oil that will ever be produced. Thanks to this viewpoint, the whole debate shifted its course from "how long will oil last?"—a question couched in reserves-to-production ratios, to "when does the peak of oil production occur?"—a question grounded in the estimate of the resources still undiscovered.

Henceforth, the size of the unknown offset the accuracy of that already known.

The basic assumptions were disarmingly simple: "in the production of any resource of fixed magnitude, the production rate must begin at zero, and then after passing through one or several maxima, it must decline again to zero" (Hubbert

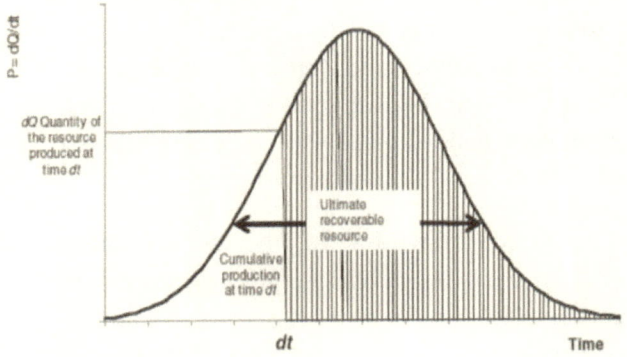

Fig. 6.3 Ultimate crude oil production according to Hubbert's logistic curve (Hubbert 1956: 22)

1956: 9). The challenge then becomes the representation of a growth curve connecting the two zeros such that the area under the curve might equal the estimate of the amount of total recoverable oil. Hubbert decided to take as his ordinate $P = dQ/dt$, in which dQ is the quantity of the resource produced in time dt, plotted against time in the abscissa. With this solution, the area under the curve at any time dt comes to represent the cumulative production up to that point.

The preference for cumulative data eased the next step of fine-tuning with Hubbert, suggesting that production over time should follow a logistic curve, and thus, yearly production should also follow the first derivative of the logistic, the bell-shaped curve. As shown in the Fig. the area under the curve corresponds to the resource ultimately recoverable.

What began at the crossroad of intuition and mathematics ended up as a blueprint to model and forecast oil depletion. The fit of the logistic curve produced from cumulative data allowed two major inferences from the process of growth in resources:

• First, the midpoint in the curve stands simultaneously for maximum production and the depletion of one half of the oil recoverable, consequently justifying the post-peak expectation of a decline in oil extraction associated with the beginning of the downward slope toward depletion.

• Second, the principle of symmetry over time, in which the production rate tends to increase exponentially during the first phase of development and is mirrored by the exponential decrease after the peak. On the microlevel, the fitness of the symmetrical form relies on the trend found in individual production fields, whose rising production stems from the high-pressure differentials of the reservoir, and whose decline is equally prompted by exponential pressure loss frequently mingled with the breakthrough of water. On the aggregated level, the fitness of the symmetrical form relies on the high probability of hitting large oilfields and speeding up the pace of discovery during initial phases of exploration, as opposed to the decreasing likelihood of such endeavors as exploration advances and the size of the ultimate recoverable resource shrinks. Symmetry results therefore from the differential probabilities of discovering oil, which determine production levels with a constant time lag (10–12 years in the USA).

Resorting to the functional form of the bell-shaped curve, Hubbert delivered some bad news and some mitigating evidence to his contemporaries: bad, because the single-peak, anticipated a turning point in the era of fossil fuel abundance, with a potential negative impact upon economic growth; mitigating, because the symmetry around the peak assured a relatively smooth transition to the period of scarcity and because the post-peak decline of fossil fuels could be overcome by a stronger commitment toward nuclear energy. Having recently discovered the magnitude of the energy that could be obtained from fission and the relative abundance of uranium and thorium reserves, Hubbert deemed it appropriate to complement the fossil fuel scenario with a convenient alternative.

Ultimately, what came to the fore and was spotlighted by the press and energy experts was the central concept of peak along with the prediction that the US oil industry might shortly enter its downward slope. Unsurprisingly, the discovery got a very cold reception, to say the least and was criticized both by executives and by government officials. The turnaround took place in 1970, when the US production of crude oil and natural gas liquids started to fall, confirming one of Hubbert's peak forecasts. Although the controversy did not come to a halt, the geophysicist was at that juncture turned into a kind of conservationist folk hero and praised even by those who had previously opposed him. The oil industry had begun to side with the peak thesis and President Carter's election, in 1977, brought conservationists into the very heart of federal government.

From its very inception, the breakthrough introduced by Hubbert stems from the representation of $P = dQ/dt$ in the graph ordinate. This idea enabled the mapping of the ratio of cumulative production to resource size through recourse to dQ expressing the quantity of the already produced resources. Hence, a key element in the overall approach turned out to be the estimation of the resource size or ultimate recoverable resource (hereafter URR). The point proved particularly sensitive since URR, or the area under the production curve, includes the oil-yet-to-be found, precisely the unknown portion of the original endowment of conventional oil. This portion has to be estimated through geological techniques of inference or through the extrapolation of production or discovery trends, when exploration is well advanced. Given the contingencies present in such assessments, one can more easily understand what was previously stated about the prevalence of the "size of the unknown" over other aspects of analysis and the revolution it provoked in the depletion debate.

Based on a track record of outstanding geological and geophysical expertise, Hubbert proposed, in 1956, an original endowment of global conventional oil (URR) of 1,250 billion barrels ($1,250 \times 10^9$). Later, other geologists made an upward revision of this ceiling and by the 1970s several independent estimates clustered around the value of 2,000 billion barrels or 2,000 Gb (the abbreviation Gb—Giga barrels henceforth designates billion barrels). Other things being equal, the greater the proposed size for the URR, the more the center of the logistic curve would be displaced toward the right, pushing further ahead the estimate of the turning point for global peak oil. The current situation can be summarized into two broad groups of forecasters: On the one hand, those forecasting an URR in the range of 1,900–2,800 Gb, implying peak oil occurring between 2009 and 2020; and on the other hand, those who estimate an URR clustered between 2,900 and 3,900 Gb that knocks the peak oil timeframe back to between 2021 and 2030. It is worth remarking that the latter group of more optimistic scenarios includes the major oil business institutions of reference, for example the International Energy Agency (IEA) of the OECD, the Energy Information Administration (EIA) of the US Department of Energy, and research departments at oil companies such as Shell, Exxon, and Statoil. Another important conclusion is that should the lower "pessimistic scenario" estimates hold true, and then, the peak has already been reached, or is rapidly approaching. The question that logically surfaces is whether or not we have already reached the peak without noticing it? From a theoretical viewpoint, the potential answer is yes: yes, we could do. Production of conventional oil has recently gone flat, with a drop in 2009, and such a scenario matches the concept of a multiyear plateau in which production fluctuates by a few percentage points before definitively entering into decline. Whatever the case, the global peak oil phenomenon is only empirically susceptible to ex-post confirmation. [1]

7.5. Peak Oil and Related Issues

The term "peak oil" expresses the idea that resources of mineral resources such as petroleum will in the near future be in short

(¹)Nuno Luís Madureira. Key Concepts in Energy. Springer International Publishing Switzerland 2014. P 119: 124

supply if not totally exhausted. As shown in the Fig. the basic idea is simple: global population is increasing

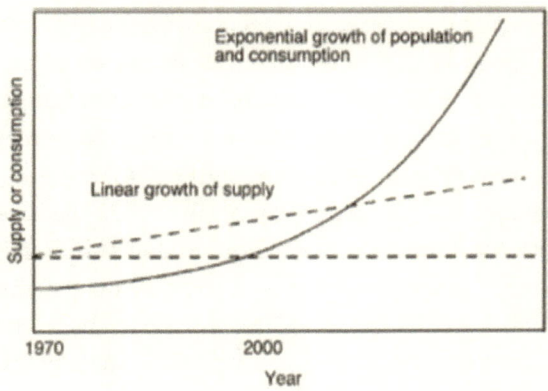

exponentially and if it continues to grow, the demands of this expanding population will inevitably consume any natural resource, which manifestly is finite.

The notion that we will run out of natural resources, including metals, is not new. Malthus, in his celebrated article written in 1798 (An Essay on the Principle of Population, as it Affects the Future Improvement of Society with Remarks on the Speculations of Mr. Godwin, M. Condorcet, and Other Writers; Malthus (1830)) predicted that the increase in human population would rapidly exhaust supplies of food and natural resources, and the theme has been revisited many times since then.

In the report of the 'Club of Rome' published as the book "Limits to Growth", Meadows et al. (1972) also used a model in which human population and consumption of resources increased exponentially while the rate of discovery of new resources increased at best linearly. The consequence, if the assumptions are correct, is rapid depletion of these resources, as shown in the Fig. According to the more pessimistic prediction made in 1972, the year that the book was published, global supplies of copper would now have become scarce, of not totally exhausted. Clearly this has not happened—copper is still mined in deposits all over the world in amounts that satisfy global demand. In 1972, the total amount of copper known to exist in clearly identified and readily exploitable deposits was sufficient to ensure supplies, at the rate of consumption estimated at that time, for only the following 21–48 years, depending on the assumptions that are made. Table 6.1 compares the predicted times before exhaustion of copper and six other metals, as estimated by Meadows et al. (1972), with another set of estimates made using recent data from the United States Geological Survey (2013). To make this estimate we simply divided the estimates of global reserves of the metal by the annual production. Despite more than 40 years of consumption, the estimated times before "exhaustion" of these metals have barely changed and in some cases, they have increased. How can this be?

One product that went through a peak of production then dramatically declined is, paradoxically, renewable. Spermaceti, a wax present in the head cavities of the

Table 6.1 Predicted lifetimes of reserves of selected metals

	Meadows et al. (1972)				USGS mineral Commodity summaries	
	Lower estimate		Higher estimate			
	Number of years (from 1972)	Year when metal becomes scarce	Number of years (from 1972)	Year when metal becomes scarce	Number of years (from 2013)	Year when metal becomes scarce
Aluminium	31ª	2003	55	2027	106	2119
Copper	21	1993	48	2020	40	2053
Gold	9	1981	29	2001	19	2032
Iron	93	2065	173	2145	57	2070
Nickel	53	2025	96	2068	36	2049
Silver	13	1985	42	2014	23	2036
Zinc	18	1990	50	2022	19	2032

sperm whale, was an important product of the whaling industry throughout the 18th and 19th centuries. It was valued as high-quality lamp oil and later used as a lubricant in several types of machine. "Peak spermaceti" occurred at the start of the 20th century when overfishing drastically reduced the number of sperm whales. As spermaceti became scarce, the price rose drastically and this led to a search for substitutes; electric lighting replaced oil lamps, and oil from the jojoba plant was used as a lubricant. The demand for the product diminished, in part a consequence of social pressure to ban or restrict whaling. Now, as stocks of sperm whale slowly rebuild, not even Japanese whalers talk of hunting them.

A parallel can be drawn with the exploitation of any natural product, including metallic ores and other raw materials as well as petroleum. Julian Simon, a vocal opponent of "peak" theories, provides another example. He noted that at the end of the 19th century, the ivory used to manufacture white billiard balls was becoming scarce and expensive. The shortage led to the development of celluloid, a cheap plastic whose widespread use helped, for a short time at least, to save elephants.

A similar dynamic has affected mineral resources. Most obvious is the continuing competition between coal, oil and natural gas as the energy source for electric power. As the price of one of these commodities rises, another with a lower price will be substituted, taking some pressure off the search for new resources. More recently, climate change issues have encouraged a move away from coal to other energy sources. Similarly, as the price of copper rises, aluminum can be used as a substitute in many of its applications, again decreasing worries about exhaustion of the resource. Even slate, a common rock, has experienced a shift in markets. In the past, it was widely used as a roofing material, but around the start of the 20th century, it gave way to other materials. No one would argue that this took place because "peak slate" had been reached. The cost and effort of constructing slate roofs could not compete with alternative roofing materials. Or, to repeat the commonly cited adage, the Stone Age did not end for want of stone.

Although there can be little doubt that the production of oil and gas will eventually pass through a peak, maybe this decade, maybe far later, it is by no means clear that the cause of the peak will be the progressive exhaustion of petroleum resources. When we wrote the first edition, we thought that the main mitigating factor would be market forces. As supply diminishes, or is perceived to diminish, prices will increase and this will inevitably, sooner or later, lead to a drop-in demand. Use of petroleum will decline as we learn to waste less energy or find alternative energy sources; and, in much the same way as pressure from public and scientific bodies led to the banning of whaling, pressure from similar sources will lead us to limit petroleum use so as to decrease the rate of global warming. Because of the damage to the global environment caused by the release of CO_2 associated with the burning of fossil fuels, many groups now advocate that even currently known resources of petroleum should never be completely exploited but should be left in the ground or used for petrochemical production. Over the long term, these factors will certainly influence global consumption of petroleum products.

It now seems more likely that many apparent peaks in production and consumption of minerals and other raw materials resulted because of exhaustion only of known deposits of the type being exploited at that time. Take the oil and gas industry as an example. When we wrote the first edition, we had little knowledge of the dramatic changes that were soon to impact on global energy resources. At that time, it was generally believed that the global rate of production would soon start to decline, if it had not already done so. Access to large petroleum resources, which were concentrated in the Middle East and in other regions of potential instability, had a major influence on global politics, and was partly responsible for the catastrophic incursions into the region by the USA.

Since then the situation has changed dramatically. New discoveries of enormous oil fields off the coast of Brazil, and the potential to find other deposits from Africa to the Arctic, suggest that the supply of conventional oil and gas was not as limited as originally thought. But the real game-changer has been the discovery of vast reserves of unconventional natural gas and oil in the USA. For much of the last decade, US authorities were preoccupied by the dependence of their country on imported natural gas, often from suppliers in unstable or politically hostile countries. They had started to build a series of new terminals to accommodate tankers that would deliver liquefied natural gas to the USA from the Middle East, Indonesia, Australia and other exporting countries. They estimated that within the decade, the USA would have to import a major portion of its natural gas. At the same time, European leaders were concerned about the dependence of their countries on imports of gas from Russia— concerns exacerbated by the pressure applied by the Russian firm Gazprom on the Ukraine and indirectly on the rest of Europe. Then, quite suddenly, technological advances allowed the extraction of gas from a new source—shale and tight (impermeable) sand. This resource had been known for over a century but previously the gas could not be extracted economically from such low-permeability rocks.

Newly developed horizontal drilling methods provided better access to flat-lying sedimentary strata, and "fracking" or hydraulic fracturing increased their permeability, allowing gas and oil to be extracted.

The huge increase in USA gas production in the last 2000s caused the price of gas to start dropping in 2008 in the USA, although it remained high in other parts of the world. Increased oil production from shales and tight sands took longer to impact the price, but by late 2014 it had declined precipitously from over $100/bbl to below $65/bbl. The USA now satisfies a much larger fraction of its domestic consumption and has returned to its earlier role as the world's biggest petroleum producer. The availability of cheap and abundant energy has boosted US industry: according to some sources, it led in 2013 to a remarkable one-percent increase in gross domestic product.

The shale and tight sand boom has been slower to impact the rest of the world Shale gas provides about 15 % of Canada's natural gas production and some shale

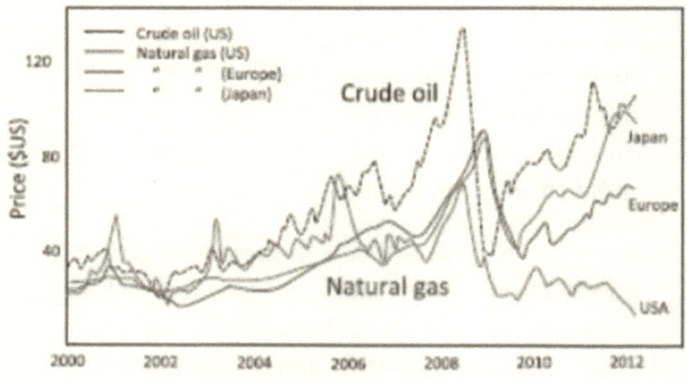

gas (<1 %) is produced in China. European countries such as Poland and Great Britain, as well as South Africa, Australia, Argentina and China, have large potential reserves of shale gas and oil, and in some of these countries steps have been taken to evaluate these resources. But in other countries, France being the prime example, vocal public opposition to the possible extraction of shale gas has led parliament to ban even the exploration for this resource. The main fuel for this opposition is environmental issues, with ecologists expressing concern about the high consumption of water, potential leaks of the chemicals used in the process, and possible contamination of ground and surface waters.

Why do we write in so much detail about shale gas and oil—a product that is somewhat apart from the main theme of this book? The reason is that the controversy surrounding the supply and demand for oil and gas, and the public perception of these issues, has much in common with the mining of metals and other mineral products. Recent changes in the global petroleum sector relate directly to the question we posed at the start of the chapter: why hasn't growing global population and growing demand for metals in developing countries already exhausted our supplies of these metals? In addition, the growing public opposition to the exploitation of shale gas in some countries finds a direct parallel in similar opposition to domestic mining. [1]

In a world without Peak Oil, the business interests of the oil industry held oil prices to a secular price between US$ 10 and 30 per barrel (2006 base year). This assured global

[1] Nicholas Arndt • Stephen Kesler Clément Ganino: Metals and Society. 2nd edition. Springer International Publishing Switzerland 2015. P 173: 178

oil addiction and little headway into developing alternative sources of energy. Peak Oil has changed the picture, but it has not negated the power or motive of the business interests of the oil industry. With more limited ability to increase supply to meet increasing demand, nonconventional oil is an essential part of the current oil mix, and it has become increasingly difficult to stabilize oil prices.

Nonetheless, the oil industry will try to do so because it is necessary to see to it that oil prices do not go so high as to destabilize the global economic system. The price of oil rose significantly and fluctuated dramatically in the first decade of the twenty-first century, but now it seems to have stabilized around US$ 100 per barrel in current dollars.

To be sure, we can point to many proximate causes of this price increase, not the least of which is political instability in the Middle East and Peak Oil. But, if we were inclined to think in broader terms, that is, based on the distinction between business and industry, it is quite possible to conclude that we have now stabilized around a new secular price of oil. Our interpretation of the price is important. It is high enough to solicit the development of oil with higher lifting costs (now a necessary addition to oil supplies), but low enough to continue to sustain our global oil addiction without altering the current economic order, and its reliance on oil. Thus, it is both strategic and an indication that we have reached a different point in our historical relationship with oil. It is a sign that we are reaching Peak Oil; but, it does not mean an abrupt end to our addiction to oil or the economic order that sustains it and gives it expression. There will be every effort made to sustain the new secular price for as long as possible. And, the new secular price of oil and the institutional realities out of which it emerges will have everything to say about our transition out of the Age of Oil.

It is not productive to characterize our present situation as an indictment of the oil industry. The oil industry is simply operating as a going business concern, and those who participate are simply doing what they are legally allowed and economically encouraged to do. As Veblen reminds us, "There is nothing gained by finding fault with any of this businesslike enterprise that is bent on getting something for nothing, at any cost. After all, it is safe and sane business, sound and legitimate, and carried on blamelessly within the rules of the game." It is much better to couch our criticism of our situation in the context of our economic order and its institutional realities.

In a rational world, where petroleum engineers were calling the shots, the production, distribution, and uses of petroleum would be far different. Would we, in such a world, even be using oil? Surely, if the control of our industrial capabilities were not under the domination of business interests, we would have begun the transition out of oil long ago. In the words of the petroleum geologist Kenneth Deffeyes, "World oil production has stopped growing; declines in production are about to begin. For the first time since the Industrial Revolution, the geological supply of an essential resource will not meet the demand. There has been plenty of warning.... Fifteen years ago, we should have started investing heavily in alternative energy strategies. That opportunity is now lost. There is no time left for scholarly research.

There is no time left for engineers to develop new machinery." The warnings could have been communicated by prices in a competitive market; but of course, they were not. But in today's world, competitive markets have nothing to do with the market economy that exists. As Walt Kelly's comic strip character, Pogo, once said, "We have met the enemy and he is us." [1]

---

[1] J. Edward Gates • David L. Trauger • Brian Czech: Peak Oil, Economic Growth, and Wildlife Conservation. Springer Science+Business Media New York 2014. P 93: 94

References

1. Alan K. Burnham: Global Chemical Kinetics of Fossil Fuels. Springer International Publishing AG 2017.
2. C.J. Campbell: Campbell's Atlas of Oil and Gas Depletion. Colin J. Campbell and Alexander Wöstmann 2013.
3. Charles A.S. Hall: Energy Return on Investment. 2017.
4. Congrui Jin • Gianluca Cusatis: New Frontiers in Oil and Gas Exploration. Springer International Publishing Switzerland 2016.
5. Ferenc L. Toth: Energy for Development Springer Science+Business Media Dordrecht 2012.
6. François Roure • Ammar A. Amin Sami Khomsi • Mansour A.M. Al Garni: Lithosphere Dynamics and Sedimentary Basins of the Arabian Plate and Surrounding Areas. Springer International Publishing AG 2017.
7. J. Edward Gates • David L. Trauger • Brian Czech: Peak Oil, Economic Growth, and Wildlife Conservation. Springer Science+Business Media New York 2014.
8. Joseph Tawonezvi: The legal and regulatory framework for the EU' shale gas exploration and production regulating public health and environmental impacts. Energ. Ecol. Environ. 2017.

9. Khalid Al Hosani • Francois Roure • Richard Ellison • Stephen Lokier: Lithosphere Dynamics and Sedimentary Basins: The Arabian Plate and Analogues. Springer-Verlag Berlin Heidelberg 2013.
10. Kirsten Heimann • Obulisamy Parthiba Karthikeyan Subramanian Senthilkannan Muthu: Biodegradation and Bioconversion of Hydrocarbons. Springer Science+Business Media Singapore 2017.
11. Kun Sang Lee • Tae Hong Kim: Integrative Understanding of Shale Gas Reservoirs. 2016.
12. Mark J.Kaiser, Brian F.Snyder: The Offshore Drilling Industry and Rig Construction in the Gulf of Mexico, Springer-Verlag London 2013.
13. Maurizio Di Paolo Emilio: Microelectronic Circuit Design for Energy Harvesting Systems. Springer International Publishing AG 2017.
14. Michael D. Max · Arthur H. Johnson William P. Dillon: Natural Gas Hydrate – Arctic Ocean Deepwater Resource Potential. 2013.
15. Nazim Muradov: Liberating Energy from Carbon: Introduction to Decarbonization. Springer Science+Business Media New York 2014.
16. Nicholas Arndt • Stephen Kesler Clément Ganino: Metals and Society. 2nd edition. Springer International Publishing Switzerland 2015.
17. Nuno Luis Madureira: Key Concepts in Energy. Springer International Publishing Switzerland 2014.

18. Patrick A. Narbel • Jan Petter Hansen Jan R. Lien: Energy Technologies and Economics. Springer International Publishing Switzerland 2014.
19. R.L.Sengbush: petroleum exploration, a quantitative introduction, library of congress 1st edition 1986.
20. R.W. Bentley: Introduction to Peak Oil. Springer International Publishing Switzerland 2016.
21. Ripudaman Malhotra: Fossil Energy. Springer Science+Business Media New York 2013.
22. Roger Boyd: Energy and the Financial System Springer Cham Heidelberg New York Dordrecht London 2013.
23. Roozbeh Khosrokhavar: Mechanisms for CO_2 Sequestration in Geological Formations and Enhanced Gas Recovery. Doctoral Thesis. Springer International Publishing Switzerland 2016.
24. Rossella Bardazzi • Maria Grazia Pazienza Alberto Tonini: European Energy and Climate Security. Springer International Publishing Switzerland 2016.
25. Sidney Borowitz: FAREWELL FOSSIL FUELS Reviewing America' s. Energy Policy. Plenum Press, New York in 1999.
26. V. Vishal • T.N. Singh: Geologic Carbon Sequestration. Springer International Publishing Switzerland 2016.
27. Xuetao Hu • Shuyong Hu Fayang Jin • Su Huang: Physics of petroleum Reservoirs, Petroleum Industry Press, Beijing, China 2017.

28. Yasar Demirel: Energy Production, Conversion, Storage, Conservation, and Coupling. Springer-Verlag London Limited 2012.

Biography of the author

Roshdy Ebrahim Abdin, Egyptian.

Ph.D (economics)

Economic lecturer.

Member at the Egyptian assembly for political economy.

Member at the Egyptian assembly for international law.

Professional diploma in arbitration.

diploma in importing and exporting.

Lawyer since 2008.

For more information please subscribe to my blog:

http://roshdyebrahim.blogspot.com.eg/

the author's books
1. Economic study of Oil and Gas Well Drilling
2. Economic study of Oil and Gas Exploration
3. Economics of oil and gas production
4. Economics of Petroleum reservoirs
5. Economics of petroleum market
6. Explanatory of petroleum market volatility

www.ingramcontent.com/pod-product-compliance
Lightning Source LLC
Chambersburg PA
CBHW031616210526
45464CB00004B/1603